To John [illegible]

With Best [illegible]

Tim [illegible]

June 3rd. 2013

TED THE LAD

A Schoolboy Who Went To War

by

Ted Cachart

Assisted by
Alan & Barbara Parr
Derek Vanstone
John Ward

ISBN - 978-0-9532252 - 3 - 1

British Library Cataloguing in Publication Data. A catalogue of this book is available bt application to the British Library

Photographs.

Except where stated in the captions attached to the photographs, the copyright of photographs used in this book belongs to Jote Publications, the 49 Squadron Association Collection or are from private sources who have given permission for their use..

Published by

Ted Cachart and John Ward trading as:-
JoTe Publications. 4 Cottage Close.
Heage. Belper. Derby. DE56 2BS

Telephone 01773 853181
Email: tedthelad@bigfoot.com

Printed

in Great Britain by the
MPG Books Group,
Bodmin and King's Lynn

First Published October 2007

DEDICATION

This book is dedicated to the memory of my very good friends 'The Three Musketeers', Tom Brady, Bill Dykes and Jimmy Goddard. They, with the 55,885 other volunteers in Bomber Command paid the ultimate sacrifice.

Their sacrifice must never be forgotten.

It is also dedicated to my wife Betty who, for forty years put up with my 'Seven year itch', the dust and rubble of various renovations of properties in which we lived and my passion for changing one car for another.

The peals of her laughter still ring in my ears.

To my children Antony and Jacqueline, grandchildren Hayley, Lucy, Edward, Emily and great granddaughter Megan.

To our pilot Johnny Young whose skill enabled his crew Jack 'Scotty' Scott, Les 'Orch' Orchard, Alan 'Vi' Vidow, Alan 'Spud' Mahony, Len Crossman and myself to live to fight another day.

Finally, to all veterans of Bomber Command and last but not least, all Ex-Prisoners of War.

ACKNOWLEDGEMENTS

This book would never have been written had it not been for the encouragement (and pressure) by my good friend John Ward, himself an author and artist and President of the 49 Squadron Association. Nor would it have been finished and published but for the help and enthusiasm given by other good friends, Alan Parr, Secretary of the 49 Squadron Association, who, with his wife Barbara did the majority of the proof reading. Derek Vanstone of Aviation Books for his support and unstinting friendship over the past six or more years, and to all the aviation enthusiasts I have met at various venues over the past 10 years who have repeatedly said "Put it in writing" - so I have.

LIST OF CONTENTS

FOREWORD

I have read many war books but "Ted The Lad" is particularly interesting as it illustrates the development of a young man through his career in the Royal Air Force and later as a civilian. It also provides a very personal story of life during World War 2.

Ted was remarkable as he falsified his age and volunteered for the RAF when he was still fifteen years old. He was soon on operations on heavily defended targets, such as Berlin, at the height of the Bomber Offensive when the casualty rate was highest. His book also brings to life many details of squadron and prisoner of war life which I had forgotten. It also mentions many members of the RAF ex-Prisoners Of War Association we have known over the years. He must have undertaken a great deal of research to be able to record so much detail of the operations in which he took part.

The book also reminds us that seventy-five per cent of the bomber crews were NCOs and were responsible for many audacious prison camp escape attempts and this is too often forgotten.

I certainly enjoyed reading Ted's book. His style makes it very easy to read and it will be of interest to all ages.

Air Commodore Charles Clarke OBE
President / Chairman
RAF ex-Prisoners of War Association.

Sgt Ted Cachart aged 17 Photo taken in spring 1943 on completion of the Air Gunnery course.

INTRODUCTION

This is not a story of brave deeds or extreme heroism, in fact it is really rather lack lustre but it is told for two main reasons. Firstly, I hope that young people by reading this, or by having their parents teach them, will realise that it is already too late when they say, **"I wish I had .... "**, and be encouraged by the following message:

"If you have a dream or desire to do something, think very carefully about it and if it is a REAL desire then DO IT TODAY. You have a vast future before you, make every day count. Take a chance and make things happen, there will be many unexpected twists and turns but that is normal in any adventurous life. Don't sit back and dream about what you might like to do, get up and do it. Tomorrow NEVER comes and you don't get a second chance to relive yesterday."

The second is more mundane; having been pestered by friends, colleagues, aviation enthusiasts and historians to 'Tell my story' before it is too late, I am following my own philosophy and doing it NOW before it IS too late and maybe some reader who, in the future, fulfils his or her dreams will think back and recall that the inspiration came from reading 'My story' and will say 'Thanks for the encouragement Ted'.

The number 13 seems to have played a part in my life, how many will you find within these pages? (excluding this one and those which are part of a larger number).

For Ted

For months and months I searched in vain,
To find my uncle, man and plane
I read a story on a site,
About a man who crashed in flight
He was from Squadron 49
Maybe I'll strike some help this time,
A request was sent across the net
And help I got from him you bet
I'll tell you now his name is Ted
We've learned a lot from what he said
What's it like in the skies to soar
What's it feel like to hear a Lanc roar
To jump out from a damaged plane
To wonder whether you'd see family again
Times in a prison camp and much more
Tales of a schoolboy who went to war.

By Sandie
For Ted
With thanks
13th Oct 2005

1

THE BOY

I was born on June 15th 1925 in the town of Gorlston-On-Sea in Norfolk, one of five children of Benjamin Newton Cachart and Dorothy Clarice Cachart (nee Roe) – Children in age order; Robert (Bob), Douglas (Doug), Barbara, Edward (Ted) and David, born later in 1938.

My father, who joined the Kings Royal Rifle Regiment in 1915, left the Army as an R.S.M in 1919 and began studying for accountancy whilst running a small shop selling toys and radios. I can just remember him charging customer's small accumulators. Yes, they used to run radios on accumulators.

After completing his training he became a Registered Chartered Accountant and in 1929 we moved temporarily into a flat in London prior to buying a house in Toorack Road, Wealdstone, Middlesex. All four children attended Whitefriars School. We moved five years later to West Avenue, Rayners Lane, Pinner. Brother Bob joined the army as a regular, Doug was working in Harrow and my sister and I attended Vaughan Road School in West Harrow, some two miles from home. We used to walk each way and occasionally would even go home for lunch which meant walking both ways twice.

A new junior school (Longfield) opened in Dukes Avenue, Rayners Lane, which was just around the corner from where I lived and I was one of its first pupils. Despite living so close I still managed to be late for school on occasions. About 15 months later, aged 11, I was transferred to Headstone Lane Senior School in North Harrow. This is now named Nower Hill School. In those days you had your 'own' classroom and a teacher who taught you the basic three R's for about a year.

We would go to other teachers for special subjects such as Science (all), Woodworking (boys) or Domestic Science (girls).

So, for the first year I had Mr 'Hoppy' Swales who also taught gardening and bee keeping. This was followed in the second year with Miss Stribley, a red haired Amazon type who thrilled us with her talks about climbing in the 'Rockies' in Canada and the USA. She also took part in sports and was a fantastic batswoman at cricket. In the final year Mr Reid, the deputy Head Master, was our tutor. It was whilst I was in his class that I obtained a scholarship at the age of thirteen to attend a 'trade' college.

At the time it was conventional for boys to go to a technical college and learn metal and woodwork, plumbing and other skills in the building trade. In my case, being the 'odd ball', I opted to train to be a chef.

I was interviewed and offered a place at the The City of Westminster Hotel and Catering College in Vincent Square, London. In the few months before I started at the College, instead of woodwork I went to domestic science classes with the girls and learned some of the basic housekeeping and cooking skills. This resulted in some of the lads making jokes and others being jealous of my good luck.

From about the age of ten I nearly always had a Saturday morning job. For a few months I worked on Saturdays with Davis's Bakery. I helped the delivery man and we covered the route with a horse and cart. I was paid two shillings and sixpence by Mr Davis and the rounds man also gave me sixpence. Each week I spent the sixpence and put the rest into a Post Office Savings Account.

Another time I helped an Express Dairies milkman. I had to meet him at the dairy at 6.30 in the morning and help load the electric float. The float was a long rectangular box shape with an open platform at the back on which you stood whilst driving. It had one forward and one reverse gear with a combined accelerator and 'dead man's brake' in the floor of the platform, lift your foot off it and the vehicle would stop. I drove both the horse and cart as well as the electric float which was great fun for a young lad. I also worked for a local butcher, grocer, ironmonger, baker, milkman and delivered papers for the newsagent. I remember one day a customer, on opening her door, looked at me and said, "What are you to-day, butcher, baker or candlestick maker?"

Despite work I still found time to enjoy myself. With a couple of friends we would 'go camping', buying bacon scraps and broken biscuits from the local Tesco shop (Yes, Tesco had small individual shops in those days) and raiding our parent's pantries for other items. We would pitch our tent in the fields about 500 yards from where we lived... not very adventurous but we enjoyed cooking our own food over an open fire and pretending we were miles away in open country.

The Cachart Children (l to r) Barbara, Ted, Douglas and Bob

At that age it was common practice to think up dares and challenges such as climbing tall trees, running over a fallen tree that formed a 'bridge' over the stream or 'tightrope' walking on the narrow wood fencing at Northolt Race Track.

Challenges were frequently made and you were a ‘sissy’ if you refused to accept one, but if you achieved it, then the challenger had to do it or be the ’sissy’. Subconsciously it taught us self confidence and decision making, learning from failing to do something right at the first, second or subsequent attempts. The many cuts and bruises received were far outweighed by the satisfaction of having ‘dared the dare’, or achieving the task.

Miss Holiday, the Head Mistress at the Longfield Junior School, was a musician and she wrote the Morning Assembly School Song. I can just remember these two lines which may have influenced me later in life;

“Perseverance helps a man along,
Cheerfulness inspires a merry song”

It was early in 1939 at the age of thirteen that training in my culinary skills commenced. It meant a 35 minute journey on the tube train which necessitated an early rise as I had to add another 25 minutes for the walk at either end. We had to purchase two complete sets of white linen jackets, trousers, aprons and tall chef’s hats, plus a set of knives that were contained in a wooden sheath hung on a wide leather belt (I still have these knives but the sheath collapsed years ago).

We had classroom lessons in the morning which included French. This was essential and with a steep learning curve as the chef tutors were mostly French and expected you to understand what they were saying. The afternoons were spent in the kitchens and for the first year training would be concentrated on patisserie and sweets. The three year course would take in similar periods on meat and fish courses. All the food we prepared was served in a restaurant which was open to the public, as well as feeding the staff and other students.

War clouds were forming and rumours were plentiful.

2

MY WAR

Although World War II started on 3rd September 1939, 'My War' began a few days before the end of August when the college, staff and students were evacuated to Brighton. The London college building was to become an emergency hospital. A train load of youngsters waved goodbye to weeping parents as we set off on a great adventure. We took our gas mask in a cardboard box slung with a string over our shoulder, a bag of personal belongings and possibly a few sweets in our pockets. There were a few who were upset by leaving home but most, like myself, could not get there fast enough, it was like a holiday at the seaside.

At Brighton we were all assembled in a park and local residents walked around examining us like cattle in a market as they selected the one or two youngsters that they would be willing to take into their home.

The Royal Pavilion, Brighton.

I was selected with one other boy by a kindly couple. He and I had to share a bed and were made to stay out of the house on Sunday afternoons when the husband had a sleep.

After two-months I opted to go home and get a job as we were not really getting the proper training due to the overcrowding and lack of facilities. We did do some training in the kitchens of the Royal Pavilion although we never actually cooked anything on the huge Regency style rotary spit installed in front of a large fireplace. This was big enough to roast a whole carcase of beef.

So, at the age of fourteen I returned home and got a temporary job as a delivery boy in a local ironmongers. They provided me with a pedal 'trade' cycle having a front carrier with the addition of a flat sidecar.

On this I made my deliveries. When empty I used to ride with the sidecar tipped up so that its wheel was in the air and with the cycle leaning to one side, much to the amusement of passers by. Was this the original Wheelie?

A few months later, as a result of writing to a number of local catering companies, I received an offer of employment with Wright Cooper in Harrow, a fairly large bakery with eight branch shops in the local area. I was to work in the cake making department starting as the 'tin boy' preparing the tins in which the cakes would be baked.

I helped empty them when cooked and then clean and grease them ready for the next batch. What with fetching and carrying things for any of the adult staff, I was also a 'Gofor'.

Fred Taylor was the charge hand over Bob Wratten, Sammy Cook and the two lads, Eddie and myself. Between the five of us we produced between 300 and 500 cakes, tarts and sponges, etc every day.

My first task every morning was to fill two large piping bags, one with whipped cream and the other with jam, and then inject a small amount of each into the hot doughnuts that had been the last items cooked by the night shift and left stacked on metal trays. When completed I had to roll the doughnuts in caster sugar and then pack them in wooden delivery trays. I was allowed to eat two every morning which I did for about ten days... then didn't eat another for many months. As in the chocolate factories, 'Let them gorge and they will stop eating soon enough.'

When Easter week began Edward and I were asked if we would be prepared to work a night shift on the Thursday night… this was actually illegal because of our young ages but the firm was suffering from a shortage of labour as men were being called up. We agreed, and after completing our normal day shift we went home, returning around 9 o'clock that evening and spending some eight hours in the third storey flour loft. Our job was to provide a steady supply of flour to the bakery on the floor below.

This was achieved by emptying the 140 pound sacks of flour into the hopper/sieve that vibrated the flour down a chute straight into the large five foot diameter mixer bowls that were wheeled into place. A cord was pulled that rang a bell in the loft telling us to tip another batch.

We went home at dawn armed with bags of hot cross buns that had been made during the night. We got double pay for (unofficial) overtime but for this night we got quadruple which was very welcome. For boys, the official union rate was four pence farthing an hour plus an added 'top up' amount agreed at the initial interview. (My 'take home pay' was twenty two shillings and sixpence.) We did get occasional bonuses but the rate for that night's work, one shilling and five pence times eight hours, was almost half a week's pay.

Mr Wright Cooper lived a few hundred yards from the bakery and on numerous occasions I had to run round before 7.30 in the morning to deliver hot croissants or bread rolls. His two sons were also directors, Mr Cyril, who, being the eldest, was in charge. His brother Richard Cooper, a well known actor who had given up the stage following an illness that had affected his walking, dealt with accounts and general administration and office duties.

Their sister was Gladys Cooper, a stage and film actress who occasionally called and would visit us in the bakehouse. On one such visit, as she walked through she saw me packing some small tarts into delivery boxes and asked if she could have one... who was I to say no!

Billy Cooper, the son of Cyril Cooper, also worked in the bakehouse. He joined the RAF shortly after I did, as a pilot. He was killed on 24th December 1943 flying on operations with 100 Squadron.

Over the next twelve months Bob Wratten was called up into the Navy and is believed to have been killed when HMS Hood was sunk. Sammy became a conscientious objector and was sent to work on a farm. Edward was transferred to another department leaving Fred and me (now aged 15) to do the same work that five of us had done previously .

This was the beginning of my lessons in self reliance and the belief that you can do almost anything if you try hard enough. I quickly learned to weigh and measure the various ingredients aided by the few weeks domestic science at school followed by several months training at Chefs College.

Under guidance from Fred I operated the electric mixers and hand weighed the mix into cake tins before placing these onto flat baking trays. There were triple ovens tiered one above the other, each about 5 feet wide, 18 inches high and 8 feet deep. The trays were pushed and positioned into the depths of the oven using a long handled spatula.

There were a few memorable occasions around that time, one being the day when I managed to carry a 112 pound sack of sugar from the stores into the bake house (loud applause), then the day I carried a 140 pound sack of flour down three flights of stairs, across the yard and into the bakehouse... (even louder applause). Previously I had dragged the sack across the floor, rolled it down the stairs and called for help to carry it into the bakery.

Probably the most memorable of all was the occasion when Fred took a week's holiday and I did THE LOT – albeit with a little help from the pastry section who brought in my ingredients from the stores when they fetched theirs. I made the mixes, weighed it into the individual tins, then positioned them in the oven. I had to get the foreman from upstairs to come and check that the cakes were cooked before removing them from the ovens. Working approximately three extra hours each day I was extremely tired at the end of each shift. Although I was getting extra pay the real 'spur' was the knowledge that I managed successfully to do what three men and two boys once did.

The company treated me very well and I made good use of the bonus that I received, putting it towards the purchase of a new bicycle.

Work started at 7.00 am and finished at 4.00 pm – during the summer of 1940 I would join up with a few friends, many of whom were still attending college, and go to the open air swimming pool in West Harrow.

This was the time of the start of the Battle Of Britain. When the air raid sirens sounded we had to get out of the water and wait until the 'All Clear' before being allowed back.

During these spells we would lay on our backs on the grass and watch the vapour trails or the flash of sunlight glinting on the wings of the fighters and bombers as they banked and rolled around the sky. Was this when the idea of joining the RAF was formed?

A typical recruitment poster

We would occasionally cycle over to RAF Northolt and sometimes be lucky enough to see the Polish Squadron Spitfires taking off or landing. When it was dark we would go to North Harrow where the army had set up a searchlight outside the Embassy Cinema. There was also a listening device to detect where in the sky the bombers were. This was a rotating platform with a vertical frame fitted with six large cones (like buckets).

These were connected to a headset... presumably the cones had microphones in them. An operator sat on the seat and was rotated with the device as he passed directions and angles to the searchlight operator. My eldest brother, Bob, was a pre-war regular soldier in the Middlesex Regiment and was at that time based at the Barracks in Mill Hill a few miles away.

He had been serving in France as a despatch rider when the engine of his motor cycle had blown up causing some facial injuries (believed to have been sabotage) and he was fortunate to have been sent back home for medical treatment only a short time before the Dunkirk Evacuation.

I used to visit him about once a month at the barracks, taking along some of the damaged cake (not deliberately damaged I assure you) from work which made me very popular with his room mates. My other brother, Douglas, had been called up into the army and passed A1. He had not told them that he had some skull bone missing from the side of his head as a result of being knocked down by a car when he was a child. When the army did discover it he was quickly down graded and denied active service.

From what they told me about the 'B & B' (bull and boredom) I decided that I would opt for the excitement and glamour that was being accorded the RAF aircrews.

On the hoardings there were large posters of 'The 'Brylcreem Boys' and one (that I have never seen since) showed a pilot in Irvin flying jacket, flying boots and carrying his helmet being followed by a line of young ladies. I think the wording was something like this:-

"Girls will queue for the boys in blue."

Little did I know that I'd be in blue sooner than expected.

The queue was noticeable by its absence.

We grew up very quickly in those early war days with adults joining up and women taking over the work that men had previously done. It was not long before youngsters were also engaged in supporting 'The War Effort'. At 14 I was a runner for the Air Raid Warden which involved taking messages from one warden's post to another. Fortunately, that area of Middlesex, west of London, had not suffered from the air raids like Central and East London, so the messages were purely an exercise in preparation for the real thing.

I also did Fire Watching which involved walking the streets for a two hour 'shift' keeping a lookout for any fires resulting from incendiary attacks etc. My usual shift was from 2.00 am to 4.00 am. On being woken by the alarm clock I would get dressed and wait outside for the person whom I was relieving.

He would hand me the whistle, torch, steel helmet and a

section of motor car tyre cut in the shape of a milkmaid's yoke to protect one's shoulders from shrapnel.

For two hours I patrolled the streets that were allocated to our section. I would then go to the house of the next 'watcher' and hand over to him before going home for a couple more hours of sleep.

Self analysis is always difficult but an insight into my attitude and how my characteristics had developed can be illustrated by an incident during my time at the bakehouse. I mentioned the flour loft, this was on the third floor and had a flat roof. In the hot weather I used to go up on the roof during the lunch break for some fresh air. On two sides there was a drop of some 8 or 10 feet to the roofs of the adjoining buildings, with a drop of about 60 feet to the road on the other two sides. There was a low parapet wall around the edge that was about 3 feet high and 11inches wide. One day, 'just to see if I could do it', I got onto the wall nearest the other roofs and walked along two sides of the rectangle. As I had not wobbled or fallen off I carried on along the two outer sides, never giving a thought that I could be killed or very seriously injured if I fell.

Similarly, in the fields close to where I lived, I used to climb to the top of a tall elm tree where I would sit in a crook of two branches and watch for a schoolgirl friend, Gladys Pickerill, to come out of her front door with her dog and begin to walk across the field towards 'my tree'. I would shin down like a monkey and meet her just as she arrived at the tree. We would then walk up to the shops for the evening paper.

Her father did not allow her to 'go out with boys' but that Christmas, accepting a dare from school friend Charlie, I knocked on their door on Christmas morning carrying a small box of chocolates that Charlie and I had bought for her as a present. From a safe distance he watched my progress, seeing the door open and me speaking to Gladys' mother before disappearing inside.

Gladys and her father were out walking the dog... her mother was quite friendly and invited me to wait for them to return. I did so with some trepidation but could hardly walk away, so I resolved to brazen it out.

When they arrived Gladys walked into the lounge followed by her father, she gasped when she saw me fully expecting her father to be angry. We were both surprised how pleasant he was toward me. After a few questions, who I was and where I lived, he disappeared leaving the two of us alone in the lounge.

Gladys was still rather nervous so I did not outstay my welcome, I took my leave bidding her parents a polite goodbye. From that day I could call round at any time and we would take the dog for walks to collect the evening paper. On occasions we even went to the cinema.

This again shows that with a little bit of spirit one can accept a challenge and overcome a fear which might only be in the mind and in reality does not actually exist. The worst that could have happened in this instance was to have been told quite firmly by her father that my friendship with his daughter was not welcome.

Charlie, who had been waiting a discrete distance away, could hardly believe that his 'dare' had turned out as it did. Me 'getting the girl' and he had paid half towards the chocolates. Whatever, it emphasises the fact that it is far better to be the one to 'get up and have a go' than to stand back and let others do it and then perhaps feel hard done by that they got the 'prize' and you didn't.

3

VOLUNTEERING

Early in March 1941, whilst cycling through Edgware on my way home from visiting my brother Bob at his regiment's base at Mill Hill, I saw an RAF recruiting office, stopped, and decided to enquire how I could make sure that I would be accepted into their ranks. The NCO explained that I could volunteer at the age of 17¼ if I got my parent's consent, then, if I passed the medical and aircrew selection board I would be called into the RAF when I was 18. He did not ask my age and I accepted the recruitment pack together with an application form and went on my way. Stopping off at the Moat Farm Recreation Ground I sat and quietly read through all the application papers and saw that, as well as the parent's consent signature for applicants under the age of 18, it had to be witnessed (I believe it said by a solicitor, policeman or clergyman). It did say that a birth certificate would not be required.

I did not make a conscious decision to 'join up now' I just, on a whim, followed my instincts and decided to get the form filled in anyway. Getting on my bike I cycled back to Wealdstone and called on a priest who knew my father quite well. I asked him if he would witness Dad's signature, explaining that it was just an application to ensure that I was called up into the RAF and not the Army or Navy (which was true). He readily agreed, but when he looked at the form he commented that my father had not signed it. I simply said, "Well he will when I get home."

With a smile the priest signed in the appropriate place and thanking him I cycled home. Later that evening I presented the form to my father, telling him the same story about it being just to make sure I would be accepted as aircrew in the RAF.

I had to explain how I had got the witness' signature in advance and he admonished me but signed without further comment. After pondering for a day or so I filled in all the relevant details and put my date of birth as 1923 instead of 1925 then posted it.

About three weeks later, in March 1941, a letter arrived requesting me to attend at Edgware Hospital for a medical examination – after being examined by nine or ten doctors I was passed as A1 and sent on my way. My father was surprised that I had been tested so soon but congratulated me on passing. Early in May another letter came with a rail warrant attached and I was to report to an address in Oxford on Saturday 11th May. This was for the interview by the Air Crew Selection Board.

To my father it all seemed to be perfectly innocent and so with a small bag of personal items I went off to catch a train to Oxford. On arrival at the station I realised that many of the passengers were there for the same reason and we were soon 'rounded up' by some RAF policemen and given directions to the building in which we would be accommodated.

I have vague memories of sleeping in a dormitory type room which I now presume was part of a college or university. There were about forty or fifty in the group and the next morning, after a briefing of what was to come, we had a written examination – followed by a couple of lectures.

The next day we waited in turn to be called in to the Selection Board. I have no idea how many officers there were or their ranks – I just answered their questions. When they asked me if I would like to be a pilot I declined as I did not consider that I had the necessary education, or that I would get away with it.

I mentioned my interest in guns (air rifle and pistol) and a little knowledge of radio and I was accepted as a trainee Wireless Operator / Air Gunner (Wop/Ag).

No mention was made about my age and I still did not know if I would be found out and sent home, but as no one asked me I just kept quiet and let things take their course. That Monday afternoon, when everyone in the group had been interviewed (I don't recall if any failed), we were gathered into a room, lined up in two ranks, given a slip of paper containing a seven digit number, told to raise our right hands and repeat the words as they were read out and we were sworn in to serve H. M. King George VI. Having accepted the 'King's Shilling' we were now Aircrew Trainees and members of the RAF.

I had previously chatted to another of the volunteers, Harry Bickell. He was standing in line a few paces on my left and we compared our service numbers, his was 1318569 and mine 1318564, just 5 difference. We later became friends as we were together on the same training courses for the first six months after being called up. (See group photo page 21) We were destined to meet up again on a number of occasions as you will see later.

This was May 13th, a month before my 16th birthday.

I only had to look at that slip of paper once and the number 1318564 was burned into my memory and never has, or ever will be, forgotten. We were told that we could expect to be called into uniform shortly after our 18th birthday which in my case would be my 16th in a few weeks time. We were also advised to join the local Air Training Corps.

My local ATC was held at my old school (Headstone Lane Senior School) and the F/Lt instructor was Mr (Hoppy) Swales, a WWI Marine veteran who had been my teacher for my first year there. He limped from a WWI injury hence the nickname ‘Hoppy’. (Not used within hearing range.)

Uniforms were rather scarce at the time and I did not push to get one as I now hoped that my devious two year age increase would not be discovered as it would have resulted in me not being around to wear it for long. In the few months that followed I learned to march, did some aircraft recognition, learned general details about the RAF, the various ranks and how to salute etc., but also, most importantly, the Morse Code in which I achieved a speed of four words per minute.

Having worked inside the hot bake house for around 15 months, the lack of exercise during the winter, the heat and the much longer working hours meant that I was not quite as fit and healthy as I would have liked. In anticipation of being ’called up’ I decided that with the summer months ahead an outside job would be good for me until that day came.

I saw an advertisement by Davis, the bakers for whom, as a boy, I had worked on Saturdays. They wanted a deliveryman. On my way home from work I called in and saw Mr Davis to discuss the vacancy. He explained that he had sacked one of the roundsmen who had been stealing customer’s payments and the ’round’ was in a mess. As he knew me and believed he could trust me despite my young age he offered me the job and I agreed to start the following week.

Some roundsmen, instead of a horse and cart, had hand drawn ones similar to the one shown in the photograph (next page). For the round that I was to take over I had the latest model hand cart of similar design but with smaller wheels with rubber pneumatic tyres and aluminium body. It was much quieter and easier to pull. These carts had a small castor wheel on a support ‘leg’ at the back to protect the body from damage if it tipped backwards. You stood between the shafts, hooked a strap around your waist and pulled with your body. You only needed to hold the shafts to maintain the balance and to guide it. The start of my round was over two miles from the depot so I had a good distance to pull at the beginning and end of each day. I soon found that by carefully adjusting the position of the load towards the back of the cart it could be so well balanced that when in the 'lifted' position for pulling there was hardly any weight on the shafts. I then found that once I got it going on a level road or downhill I could run with it, taking loping strides of about six to eight feet between each foot touching the ground, my weight being taken by my arms pressing down on the shafts and offset by the counter-balanced body. I used to get many a smile from pedestrians as I passed them 'loping' down their road.

For the first two weeks I asked each customer how much they owed, or when and what did they last pay. As I was new to them it came out as a natural remark and of course they did not know that it was not already in the 'rounds book'.

After each call I entered the details in the book and within a week it was all in order.

I must have walked or ran six or more miles daily and by the time my call up papers arrived I was in excellent health and as fit as I would ever hope to be.

Baker's hand cart. Courtesy www.uk-classics.co.uk

4

THE CALL UP

When my mobilization papers arrived at the end of September 1941 my father was rather cross when he learned that I had given a false age and I had to be very persuasive before he finally agreed. He was sure that I would be asking him to get me out by Christmas. I guess that I was being selfish in a way as my two elder brothers were already in the army, my sister was about to join the WAAF and here was I trying to go before my time.

However, the decision was made. I sold my pedal cycle to add to my meagre savings and said goodbye to my friends, some of whom jested that I would be kicked out and be back within a month. I got a very favourable progress report from the ATC (thanks to Hoppy) and with my treasured call up papers and Rail Warrant clutched in my hand it was with great excitement and anticipation that I left home.

I travelled by train on my own and duly reported to RAF Padgate in Lancashire. There seemed to be hundreds of us and all complete strangers, but with a common aim. We helped one another to adjust our uniforms, getting tips from others who had worn them in the ATC or in a couple of cases from men who had re-mustered from the army. We checked all the kit that we had been issued and learned what the various items were and when or how to use them. We had numerous inoculations with blunt needles, vaccinations and lectures on venereal diseases and other medical issues. Although this was my first time on an RAF base I have no recollection whatsoever of the type of accommodation we lived in for those few days.

We were next shipped off to Blackpool where, in small groups, we were accommodated in boarding houses. The landladies now housed and fed us. It was the luck of the draw as some were very supportive and others not. This period required a lot of personal adjustment, learning to share a bedroom with five or six other men and endeavouring to keep up with them in training so that my real age did not make me conspicuous (greatly assisted by my current state of fitness). As 'rookies' we soon learned what we should and should not do, albeit the hard way, being caught making mistakes and shouted at by the corporal in charge.

We were formed into squads of about thirty and marched everywhere in ranks of three abreast be it to the converted tram sheds at the south shore where we did our Morse training or the Stanley Baths at the North Shore for swimming (the sea was far too cold for that).

Drill was practised along the promenade with physical training at the huge Stanley Park. They may call the sea blue, but at Blackpool there was more blue on the land - everywhere you looked there were thousands of trainees in uniform.

Some of the Instructor's language was also blue.

When marching in the dark the outside man at the front carried a white hurricane lamp and the outside man at the rear a red one - but due to petrol rationing and the small number of car owners there was very little traffic to worry us.

Amongst many memories; mouths watering from the rich sweet smell when we marched past the toffee factory and the haircuts by supposed 'barbers' that made us look as if a pudding basin had been put on our head and every bit of hair showing below it cut and shaved off. The Morse tests held in Burtons Ball Room above the tailor's shop and the stiff shirt collars which a Chinese laundry did for us - I believe that they

The Squad. Blackpool 1941. (All from the left / front) I am 3rd in 2nd row. Johnny Nelson is 6th in 3rd row. Harry Bickell is 3rd in back row.

used rice water. Whatever it was, it gave a hard glossy surface that could be wiped clean with a damp cloth and would last for a few weeks. The concerts in the Winter Gardens - I believe Vera Lynn was in one of the shows, certainly we had a selection of celebrities to entertain us. We were always on the go, marching everywhere and with this intermixed with plenty of drill and physical training, we were ALWAYS HUNGRY!

During the three months at Blackpool we practised our Morse daily in the tram sheds. They were cold and draughty without any form of heating. We wore our overcoats but still our feet were freezing from the cold and damp concrete floor. Woollen gloves made the writing and keying very difficult so bare cold hands was the only way to operate.

A training type Morse key.

Morse code in plain language was sent using paragraphs and phrases from newspapers, any book, or other printed text. One that I often sent was a poem that I presumed had been written on the pine surface of the table by a trainee who had passed through before us. I can only remember this small part and would like to know the rest should any reader know it.

ODE TO A Wop/Ag

Not for him, the front page news
Nor does his face reflect the same
To him an 'Op' is just a cruise
A trip out there and back again

No silver wings adorn his chest
He leads no squadron into flight
His job is to control the waves
That guide them safely through the night

I believe the last line was, '*The brave and gallant Wop/Ag*'.

Just before Christmas I passed my 12 words per minute test and along with Harry Bickell and a few others I was granted my first seven days leave. We caught a train to London arranging to meet in a week's time.

I felt so proud when I walked to my home from the station in my uniform with an Aircrew Trainee white flash in my forage cap and carrying my kit-bag over my shoulder as I had seen my brother Bob do so many times when he came home on leave. This was to be the only Christmas that I had with my family during my RAF service.

5

YATESBURY

The leave seemed to pass very quickly and it didn't seem long before I was meeting the lads at the railway station. We travelled together to the Number 2 Radio School at RAF Yatesbury near Calne in Wiltshire.

This was a large camp with row upon row of long wooden huts in which to sleep. These had ablutions at the one end where the water was always cold or at best, tepid.

Other huts were our classrooms in which we learned how a radio worked and continued gaining speed with sending and receiving Morse Code.

At lunch and tea time it was always a race to be at the head of the queue so that you could eat your meal before they finished serving and then get back on the end of the queue for 'seconds'. To achieve this, a few of us made sure that our large china mugs holding our 'shifting irons' (knife, fork and spoon) were positioned ready on the shelf in the bedside locker to be grabbed as we sped past. I have to admit that I nearly always got a share of 'seconds' especially if it was something that I liked, and there was not much I didn't like.

Although I had seen Spitfires and other aircraft at RAF Northolt, these were in the distance. Bearing in mind that we were Aircrew Trainees, so far we had never been close to any aeroplane, so we were all very thrilled one day when a twin engine Westland Whirlwind beat up the Radio School. This was a streamlined twin engine fighter bomber. It looked very low as it sped along the avenue between the huts and it zoomed up with engines roaring, banked round and dived down for a second pass in the opposite direction.

A Westland Whirlwind

Anyone who served at Yatesbury will certainly remember the seemingly never ending supply of sausages and bacon that were served in the dining hall. Harris, the well known sausages makers and bacon curers, had their factory just down the road in Calne. Whether Harris were being generous with the ration issue or there was some 'back door' trading going on, we will never know. As for those that smoked, and a very large number did, they will remember popping out to the very smoky toilet block for a 'quick one'.

Another very clear memory at that station was the pay parade. When my name was called I marched up to the table, saluted the officer and said, "564 Cachart SIR", (564 being the last three digits of my service number) and collected my pay with the other hand.

After a few weeks we were told, "Do not salute the officer, stand to attention give your last three and name, take your pay and then turn smartly to the left and bow your head to Sgt John Hannah VC." He was a

No 2 Radio School Crest

Sgt Wop/Ag who was spending some time at the camp, possibly as a morale booster, but that was the ONLY time that we did not salute for our pay.

Sgt John Hannah won his VC on 15th September 1940 flying on operations in a Hampden bomber of 83 Squadron, Bomber Command.

The course was completed towards the end of March 1942 with Morse speed achieved of 22 WPM in plain language and 25 WPM in code. We proudly sewed our 'sparks' badge onto the sleeve of our uniform. This made us the only 'tradesmen' who were also aircrew. Ground staff who re-mustered to flight engineers were not granted that distinction by the RAF.

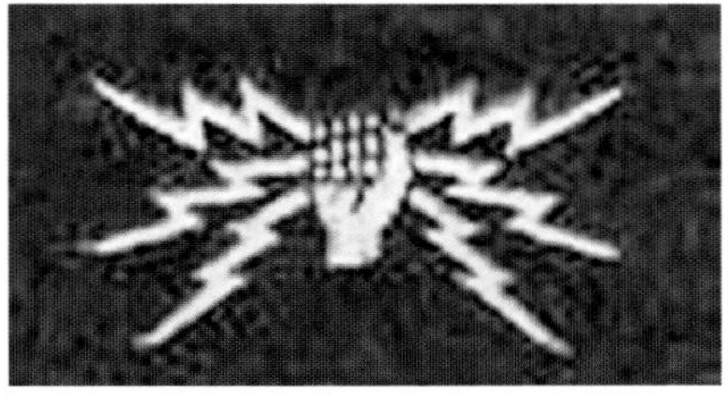

Wireless Operator's 'Sparks'

We got an increase in pay from two shillings and sixpence a day to four shillings.

We should, in theory, have then been posted to a flying school where we would practice our radio techniques in the air. However, due to the bottleneck caused by bad weather that restricted flying we were dispersed to various RAF Stations to **'make ourselves useful'**.

Barbara Cachart

Another seven days leave which coincided with my sister Barbara, the fourth member of my family to join up in H.M. Services, being on her first leave from the WAAF.

So, for the first, and as it turned out the only time, I saw her in uniform. We were able to compare notes about our respective services and the treatment, training etc. Being three years older than me she had always played ‘the big sister’, telling me what I should or should not do, and despite the fact that compared to me she was a ’sprog’, she still attempted to give me advice on RAF matters.

During this leave I spent some time with Pete Kearsey who lived about a mile from my home. We had both been on the same course together. We paid a visit to the ATC at my old school on the Sunday morning where we were made very welcome. We did not need much persuading to show off by demonstrating the fast Morse that we could now send and receive, the cadets as well as the instructor were impressed.

I recall that we popped into the Headstone Hotel for a mid-day drink. As we were not regulars and a bit hesitant about going into the main bars, we chose the small ‘snug’ where we ordered and paid for two half pints of beer. We were served by an Irish barmaid named Kitty who also served customers in the two bars on either side of the ’snug’. Every time she walked through from one bar to the other she topped up our glasses free of charge. I think that this was the first time that being in uniform resulted in someone treating us as ‘special’.

***Note.* The "Sparks" badge is unique in the RAF and it held a special place in our hearts. In the early days of the RAF an airman was not allowed to speak directly to an officer, only an NCO was permitted to do so. As wireless was introduced it was often necessary for airmen to approach an officer directly with an important signal. The "Sparks" badge was the airman's authority to approach an officer. This badge is unique as it was the first and only trade badge to be authorised by the Royal Air Force (19th September 1918 - AMO 1066) and to this day the signals trade group is the only one in the R.A.F. that has been granted the privilege of wearing a trade badge.**

6

MAKING OURSELVES USEFUL

The leave ended and once again I was on my way to pastures new. My next adventure would become the second most memorable period of my whole RAF career; this was my '**Make yourself useful**' posting.

I was very fortunate that this posting was to a Tow Target Flight based at RAF Warmwell, a fighter station near Weymouth in Dorset. Here I was to assist in the wireless maintenance section that consisted of one Canadian corporal in a small room at the end of a hut which we called 'our workshop'. The flight consisted of Lysander aircraft (I think there were four) modified for towing tubular canvas 'target' drogues on a long cable. The aircraft flew along the stretch of coastline called Chesil Beach to the west of Portland Bill. The drogue was winched out on a wire (I believe some 300 to 400 feet) and four Spitfires or Hurricanes would come zooming from inland, shooting at the drogue as they flew out to sea.

Each fighter would have different coloured paint on its bullets which enabled the number of hits for each individual aircraft to be recorded. The drogue would be winched back in and dropped though a hatch in the floor onto a nearby field where two airmen waited in a hut. They would collect the drogue then count and record the scores (if any). A second drogue would be attached and winched out again for another group of fighters. On each trip as many as four drogues might be used.

As I was the only aircrew trainee on the flight, the white flash in my cap caught the attention of the adjutant, a Polish Flying Officer, who, like some others on the flight was a fighter pilot either resting or being punished for some low flying or other prank. He called me into his office and quizzed me as to what the white flash meant and immediately said, "When I fly, you fly." The very next morning he had me kitted out with flying gear and took me up for a flight in the single engine Miles Master.

My first time in an aeroplane and a fairly fast one to boot, WOW!

He threw it around the sky doing all sorts of aerobatics. When we landed I was sick... breakfast that morning had been diced kidney in gravy. It was the only time I was ever air-sick. I am certain that the kidney was 'off' - well that's my story and I am sticking to it.

Miles Master Courtesy Eastern Express

The adjutant said that I could also fly as a drogue operator. There followed two training trips with the regular operator, Bill (I can't remember his real name). I was squeezed into the rear cockpit of the Lysander with the drogues.

Bill demonstrated how to attach and detach the drogue and how to roll it up ready to be dropped through the hatch when

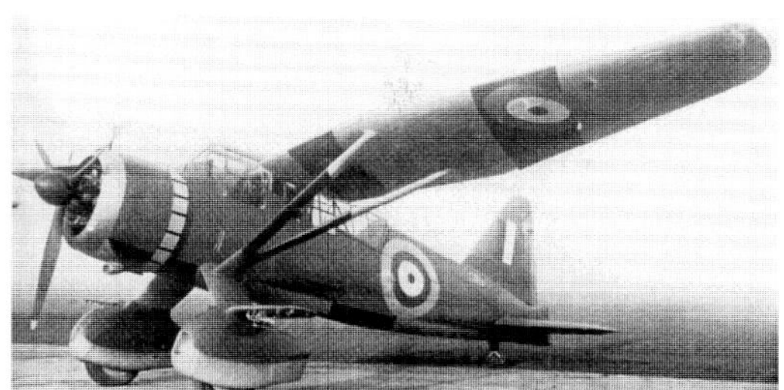

Westland Lysander 'Tug'

the pilot gave the order. From then on, although unofficial, I did the flying and Bill drew the few pence a day flying pay.

We also towed targets for the Royal Naval MGB's that were stationed at Portland. This was made more precarious due to the choppy seas making the boat rock and roll.

There were occasions when bullet holes were found in the canvas of the tail plane. I only did one trip for the MGB's but there were no holes on that one so I cannot claim to have been shot at by the Navy.

The flying was a great treat and I loved every moment of it. The real highlights were the few flights I had in the Miles Master when the adjutant would shoot up his girlfriend's farmhouse, or when he did some very low flying along Chesil Beach, heading towards Portland, pulling the nose up to soar over 'The Bill' and down again over Weymouth Bay, then up over the cliff and down into Lulworth Cove.

Boy's Own Comic exploits being carried out for real !

Ted aged 16 at RAF Warmwell. Dorset 1942

The station's tank of aircraft fuel was stored above ground with sloping sides covered in turf for camouflage and a concrete flat top with a low parapet wall. A fuel tanker was filling up one day when the hose connection leaked and burst into flames. Bill and I were just passing at the time... we rushed into the nearby hut, grabbed fire extinguishers and ran up the bank and over the parapet where we directed the foam over the bowser driver who was lying on the ground engulfed in flames. Two other airmen then rushed in and pulled the driver to safety, rolling him over to douse the flames.

He was rushed to hospital in an ambulance and later in the day it was announced over the Tannoy that he was ok but had suffered severe burns. The fire tender arrived and managed to quell the flames from the leak. The fire crew closed the valves and the bowser was towed away. We were commended by the firemen for the quick action that we had taken. They then pointed out the possibility that the entire fuel tank could have exploded with us on its roof which neither of us had even considered.

It was always a thrill to see the Spitfires and Hurricanes coming into land. Their usual direction was just a couple of hundred yards from our huts. They would appear with wheels and flaps down as they crossed the hedge and touch down on the grass. So much more exciting than the times we stood at the fence at Northolt and could only watch from some distance away.

By my 17th birthday in June that year, although unofficial and not recorded in a log book, I had achieved some 50 hours flying. Many years later when I was interviewed on Radio Derby and asked if I was scared, my reply, said without hesitation was:-

"No, I would have paid THEM to let me do that. "

7

LONDON POSTING

Sadly, my 'Warmwell holiday' was about to end. In August 1942 I was posted to South Kensington in London for a three month radio course. This was an excellent posting as it was only about 30 minutes by tube train to my home so I was able to go there at least one evening each week and most weekends. Now there's a strange thing that only occurred to me as I was typing that last piece. I could not wait to get into the RAF and here I was with the idea that I could get away from it almost any evening in the next three months.

We were accommodated in Albert Court, a block of flats behind the Albert Hall, and our dining room was in the Royal

Albert Court - A most desirable residence for aircrew trainees
Photograph supplied by Hakon Olsson, M.D. of First Penthouse Ltd.

College of Arts. Our 'school' was the Science Museum and I believe our NAAFI was in the Imperial College.

We played sports and drilled in Kensington Gardens where the tarmac road in the park was just wide enough for us to march three abreast. One day, as we approached a small bridge over a culvert a young lady walking her dog began crossing from the opposite side.

Patricia Roc

The corporal in charge called us to a halt on our side of the bridge. We stood there at attention to allow her to cross over.

As she walked past us she gave a great big smile and said:-

"Good morning boys" - it was then that we recognised her... Patricia Roc, the extremely attractive and popular film actress of that time.

Every morning we formed up (in squads of about 30 men) in front of the Albert Court in Prince Consort Road and when all were present the Duty Officer would dismiss us. We would then march to wherever we were scheduled to go, the Science Museum for classes or to Kensington Gardens for drill or physical training.

On one day a week the Commanding Officer would take the parade. In our squad we had two chaps who had re-mustered from the Army, one was a former sergeant drill instructor. He, together with the corporal who was in charge of us, taught us to drill smartly and in step with arms swinging accurately wherever we marched. There was some resentment at first but gradually pride took over and we began to enjoy it.

Our smart drill had been noted by one officer who brought it to the attention of the C.O. The next time he took the parade our squad was called to attention and marched down the whole length of the parade giving a sharp 'eyes right' as we were saluted by the C.O. A real pat on the back for us but all due to the sergeant in our ranks.

In bad weather we would use the Albert Hall for physical exercise. On one occasion there were actors on the stage, one of whom came over and asked the corporal if we would mind being quiet whilst they rehearsed.

Leslie Howard

He explained that they were giving a performance in a few days time and only had this one day when they could use the hall. It was none other than Leslie Howard, the famous film star and actor. We sat in silence watching the cast rehearse, decidedly more enjoyable than physical training.

This radio school had previously been for direct entrant wireless and electrical mechanics, consequently the staff were not used to dealing with us 'old sweats'. Problems arose quite quickly with us finding ways and means of getting past the service police if returning late or trying other dodges. In an attempt to get us to 'toe the line' they changed the latest time for returning at night from 23.59 to 22.30 - this almost caused a riot - nearly every blackboard in every class room had these words written on it. **"WE WANT 23.59."**

When we entered the museum after morning parade it had been common practise as we trudged slowly up the stairs to chant very quietly but because of the large number of voices the sound was almost deafening;

"I's a comin', I's a comin', and my head is bended low,

I hear those Angels voices singing, poor old Joe."

(The inference being that Germany had just invaded Russia and 'Joe' Stalin was now our ally).

The staff tried to stop the chanting but there were too many of us against so few of them. It got so bad that a new Squadron Leader was appointed in charge of discipline and to help him they posted in Flight Sergeant Souty (that's the nearest that I can guess the spelling of his name). We all knew him from Blackpool where he was the Senior NCO in charge of discipline... he scared the living daylights out of us as new recruits. On his first day he assembled us all at the rear of the Albert Hall. Two corporals helped him to climb up on the top of a telephone box and standing legs akimbo he shouted to us to be quiet. Then to our surprise he said (my words not his, but the meaning is correct),

"You all know me and I know that you have been in the mob for a year or more, served on various stations and think you know all the ropes and dodges - I know them better than you - so, if you want to get away early AND you have a good enough reason, come and see me and get a haircut chit. If you come back late, **don't get caught."**

As he climbed down he got a loud cheer from everyone.

Later that day, the Squadron Leader gave us an informal lecture in the dining room and I remember word for word his final statement, "You play ball with me and I will play ball with you," - and he did. Within a week the 23.59 curfew was restored and peace reigned, with very few of us being put on charges for minor offences.

There were too many of us to be able to form football or rugby teams so we devised a game where there would be about 20 or 30 on each side - a form of rugby but with a football and no holds barred. Bodies piled on top of bodies in many a wild scrum and minor cuts and bruises were common. These were a good excuse to 'report sick' and avoid a boring lesson. The Medical Officer decided that enough was enough. He decided that we should play conventional rugby from then on and he would join us and give instruction. This meant, that with only 15 a side, only half of one and half of another squad could play and all the others had to be spectators.

It quickly resulted in a number of broken bones, some were quite serious. Within a few weeks, by mutual consent, we went back to our own game which might be rougher but more fun; more bods could be involved and no serious bone breakages ensued.

T1154 transmitter T1155 receiver

This course was part refresher and part introduction to new equipment, the main item being the Marconi T1154 / R1155 transmitter and receiver. More powerful than the antiquated T1182 / R1183, it was very modern and easy to tune with the ability to pre-set frequencies that could be changed by just turning two matching coloured knobs on the transmitter to predetermined 'click stops'. This meant that you could change frequency in seconds and by counting the 'clicks' it could be carried out in complete darkness.

It was here at South Kensington that I first met three other trainee Wop/Ags; Tom Brady, Bill Dykes and Jimmy Goddard. They were already good friends having trained together at Blackpool and Yatesbury. Our paths may have crossed at various times as we were all on the same courses, but in Albert Court we were in adjoining flats and soon became good friends.

This friendship could be likened to the story of the 'Three Musketeers' with Tom as Athos, Jimmy as Porthos and Bill as Aramis. I would have been D'Artagnan, the 'oddball or upstart' who joined them later.

The three Musketeers and D'Artagnan

It might be an apt description of me but I doubt that the RAF would approve of the style of dress. It would have raise a few eyebrows if we went on guard duty dressed as in the picture, though the rapiers might have been more effective than a rifle with no bullets.

We all had to do a spell of guard duty at weekends and as luck would have it I drew the 'short straw' and was on duty for both Christmas and Boxing Day, so was unable to spend it with my family as I had hoped. The course ended about the third week of January 1943 and we had a few days leave before all meeting up again at our next posting.

8

MADELEY & WIGTOWN

This was to No 4 Radio School at RAF Madeley in Herefordshire for our flying training course to be carried out on De Havilland Dominies and Percival Proctors that were still equipped with the earlier model radios T1082/ R1083.

De Havilland Dominie

I only have a vague memory of this course. I recall being bounced around the sky in the back seat of the Proctor and trying to plug in the correct coils of the radio. This equipment had a case of tuning coils, pairs of which had to be plugged in for a particular frequency and replaced when you had to change frequency - not the easiest of tasks in such a small confined space.

Percival Proctor

With eight flights in Dominies and ten in Proctors the course was soon over and we then went 'over the border' to No.1 (O) A.F.U. RAF Wigtown in Dumfries. The Ansons were fitted with the new Marconi T1154/R1155 radios.

We quickly learned to operate these in the air. My log book shows I did just **13*** flights in the Ansons on this course. In the four weeks that we were there we became quite competent as they were so easy to set up and work.

Avro Anson

It was there that one night I sat in a Blackburn Botha with the engines running ready for the take-off when the trip was cancelled. This may have been fortunate as the Botha had a reputation for unreliability and nobody liked to fly in them.

On a warm sunny Sunday in April, Tom and I decided to go for a swim in the small river that was close to the town.

On the river bank we stripped off and in our football shorts walked into the water. It was FREEZING COLD (there were still signs of snow on the hills) but we managed to grin and bear it for about five minutes, then with faces glowing and swinging wet towels and shorts we strolled through the town.

We made our way to a private house that opened its front lounge to the RAF on Saturdays and Sundays. They served fried egg on toast with a mug of hot tea for one shilling. We joined the usual queue waiting patiently for a seat.

This course ended on 28th May. We were given 7 days leave and with the three Musketeers as company I took the train to London, dropping Bill off at Nottingham on the way.

9

GUNNERY SCHOOL

Our final posting, as Aircraftsmen (or AC Plonks), on April **13th*** was to the No. 7 Air Gunnery School at RAF Stormy Down, near Porthcawl in Wales. This was a two week course where we learned the workings of the Browning .303 guns that were used in aircraft turrets. We were taught to clear blockages and to strip and reassemble them blindfold. Why they called it an Air Gunnery School we never found out as we never went near an aeroplane.

We did do aircraft recognition and clay pigeon shooting. The climax was in a turret mounted on a stand where we were allowed to fire 200 rounds from twin Brownings at an 8 foot wooden aeroplane that went round in a circle on a track. My log records that I also fired 100 rounds at night but I have no memory of this at all.

Sgt Ted

On the 28th April 1943, aged 17, after more than 18 months training, I was promoted to Sgt Wireless operator/Air gunner, possibly the youngest in the RAF. This has never been substantiated or disputed.

We were all given seven days leave but had no idea where the next posting would lead to - Bomber or Coastal Command were the most obvious possibilities.

A bunch of newly promoted Sgt Wop/Ag's travelled by train to London where we said our farewells to friends with no idea if and when we would see each other again. Then I was onto the tube and home to Rayners Lane.

As I walked from the tube station - feeling very proud with my new sergeant's stripes and air gunner's brevet adorning my uniform, I saw, walking towards me a most attractive young lady. It was Doreen Lundy, the daughter of a neighbour.

We knew one another but as we had attended different schools we had hardly ever spoken - she smiled then stopped and said, "Hello"- I also stopped (naturally!), placed my kit bag on the pavement and we chatted a while. Being only five months younger than me she expressed her surprise that I was in uniform and already a sergeant. After answering her questions I willingly accepted her invitation to go round later for tea and to say hello to her mother. I walked on home, perhaps with a little more spring in my step.

Doreen Lundy- Photo. HMV

Back home I unpacked my kit, brought my parents up to date with my exploits and assured them once again that I was not yet flying on operations. They asked the inevitable question when you came home on leave.

"When are you going back?"

The question was never,

"How much leave have you got?"

Later, when freshened up, I called at Doreen's house. Her mother invited me in. As the three of us sat chatting and knowing Doreen and I were of similar age, Mrs Lundy enquired how it was that I was in the RAF so soon. Having explained my 'white lies' she then asked, **"When are you going back,"** the second time in a matter of a few hours -

Talk about making you feel welcome!

Mrs Lundy disappeared into the kitchen returning with a tray and passed me a cup of tea and a plate with a slice of cake that was still warm. Doreen said her mother had baked it specially as I was coming. It was a caraway seed cake and I normally hated caraway seed but politely ate the cake which in fact was quite nice being so fresh. Tea finished, Doreen's mother got up, sat at the piano and began to play. Doreen stood beside her turning the music and singing a couple of songs then, warmed up, and in a surprisingly strong voice she sang 'Ave Maria', it was so very moving and beautiful. I later learned that she hoped to make singing her career.

We went out together a couple of times but with both my brothers on leave at the same time I naturally spent most of my time with them as an 'equal' rather than the 'baby brother' as in the past.

My younger brother, David, was just five years of age and as he barely knew his three elder brothers he was somewhat shy at first but within a few days he was like a puppy, following us everywhere, wanting to be with us the whole time. It was one of the best leaves of all time, warm weather, brothers in arms spending time together, socialising and discussing experiences and meeting up with many old friends.

I also had a new friend, Doreen. The photograph was, I believe, taken just after the war and is used with the kind permission of HMV Archives.

Mrs Lundy presented me with a pair of miniature Dutch wooden clogs which I secured to the collar of my battle dress alongside the emergency whistle. Doreen, not to be outdone, gave me a square red silk scarf. These were 'good luck charms' and whilst I was not really superstitious, to please the ladies and not to tempt fate I wore both whenever I flew.

Dear reader, please remember this red silk scarf.

By post, I received a rail warrant and instructions to report to No 30 OTU (Operational Training Unit), RAF Hixon, Staffordshire. I managed to make contact with the other 'Three Musketeers' and to my surprise and joy they had all been given the same instruction. I arranged to meet Tom and Jimmy in London to catch our train to Stafford where we would meet Bill who was travelling from Nottingham. This enabled us all to check in together with the likelihood of all sharing the same billet.

The Three Musketeers

1319845
Sgt Thomas G Brady
Wop/Ag
'Musketeer Athos'

Unfortunately a photograph of Bill Dykes could not be found before publication.

1575431
Sgt William A Dykes
Wop/Ag
'Musketeer Aramis'

1319846
Sgt Alan A F Goddard
Wop/Ag
'Musketeer Porthos'

10

RAF HIXON CREWING UP

The leave was quickly over and as arranged I met Tom and Jimmy in London and caught the train to Stafford. Luckily, we were able to share a compartment and were soon settled in, making ourselves comfortable and speculating on the next part of our training. We met Bill at Stafford and with some others climbed aboard an RAF bus that was there to meet us. Hixon was equipped with Wellington twin engine bombers nicknamed 'Wimpeys'. Here we would form a crew of five consisting of pilot, navigator, bomb aimer, wireless operator and rear gunner.

The method was to put everyone into a large room and let them sort themselves into crews. Pilots wandered around talking to anyone they liked the look of and would invite them to be a member of his crew. In my case, I was approached by two Canadians. The pilot, a Flying Officer, introduced himself as John Young and his navigator as Jack Scott, after a short chat he invited me to join them. The three of us then found an English bomb aimer, Sgt Les Orchard and rear gunner, Sgt Len Crossman.

The full details of 'my' crew are:-

Pilot	J21367	F/O	JEM	Young	RCAF
Navigator	J20898	F/O	JM	Scott	RCAF
Bomb Aimer	174684	P/O	LM	Orchard	RAF
Wop/Ag	1318564	Sgt	EB	Cachart	RAF
Rear Gunner	1813501	Sgt	L	Crossman	RAF

The others were crewed up as follow:-

Tom's crew:-

Pilot	R109235	F/Sgt	CJE	Kindt	RCAF
Navigator	R148889	F/Sgt	JRR	Small	RCAF
Bomb Aimer	R153012	Sgt	AS	Macdonald	RCAF
Wop/Ag	1319845	Sgt	TG	Brady	RAF
Rear Gunner	1851986	Sgt	F	Matthews	RAF

Bill's crew:-

Pilot	R141695	F/Sgt	FFG	Allan	RCAF
Navigator	J85960	P/O	JJ	Yelland	RCAF
Bomb Aimer	R165160	F/Sgt	FI	Hughes	RCAF
Wop/Ag	1575431	Sgt	WA	Dykes	RAF
Rear Gunner	1818912	Sgt	A	Rose	RAF

Jimmy's crew:-

Pilot	J20211	F/O	GC	Bailey	RCAF
Navigator	1336990	Sgt	PD	Pick	RAF
Bomb Aimer	US10601395	Sgt	WE	Steeper	USAAF
Wop/Ag	1319846	Sgt	AF	Goddard	RAF
Rear Gunner	1874067	Sgt	RE	Locke	RAF

(Both pilot and bomb aimer of Jimmy's crew were Americans who had joined the RCAF, later transferred to the USAAF but still flew with the RAF). Of these twenty men, eight were Canadian and two American.

We flew the Wimpeys with screen instructors (experienced) on circuits and bumps followed by cross country exercises, then on our own for approximately three months, honing our skills we learned to work as a team and knitted together as a crew. Radio silence, except for an emergency, was the order of the day when flying. The obvious reason being the chance that German listening stations could pick up the transmissions.

We 'Musketeers' devised a code between us and selected an agreed HF frequency that we would all listen to whenever we were flying (but when not actually doing our normal duties). It would be a quick dit dit from me on the Morse key, a dah dah from Tom, a dit dah from Jim or a dah dit from Bill - just hearing the response was gratifying in the knowledge that our radios were correctly tuned and we had 'friends in the air with us'. No revealing call signs or messages. It was completely unofficial although all our skippers knew that we were doing it. The transmissions were so short that no one 'scanning the dial' would have had time to hear it before it was finished. We might do this a few times during a cross country especially at night when the sky seemed to be a very lonely place. Wireless operators at ground stations and control also had similar unofficial little 'codes'. Usually this was an 'extra' few key clicks after an official message such as dit - dit dit - dit with a dit dit in return.

There was a 'social night' in the Sergeants' Mess and a group of us got chatting to some local girls and at the end of the evening Tom and I agreed to walk some of them home.

We all strolled arm in arm down to the railway station and waited on the platform for their train. It departed leaving just two girls behind who lived locally. One, Olive Pye, only lived across the road from the station so she and I said we would wait whilst Tom walked her friend to her home nearly a mile down the dark lane.

Olive and I sat on the platform seat chatting as we watched the night flying aircraft coming into land from a cross country exercise. Then suddenly, one overshot the field and crashed into the rail embankment about 200 yards from the platform and one engine burst into flames. Olive ran home to telephone through to the camp and I ran, being joined by Tom who had run the last few hundred yards having heard the crash, to see if there was anything we could do.

There was no sign of any survivors, we ran around to the side not on fire and still no one. Suddenly this side also burst into flames from the leaking fuel and the whole fuselage was soon a blazing inferno with bullets exploding from both the front and rear turrets.

The fire tender arrived and as they prepared to spray foam they asked about the crew. We could only say that we had seen no-one get out. They fought desperately to get the fire under control, achieving this in about an hour or so, and we ventured into the burnt remains - there were no signs of bodies anywhere. Both Tom's and my 'Best Blues' were soaked and stained with foam and oil etc.

The fire tender gave us a lift back to the late night canteen for a well earned tea break and sitting there laughing and joking were the crew from the crashed plane. They had jumped out of the far side and run like rabbits away into the darkness from the crash. We could not see them from the side we approached because of the fire.

It was common practice for all crew members to swap 'jobs' so that in the case of anyone being injured they may be able to take over. The most important of these was taking over as pilot. We all took turns, using the dual controls, and learned how to fly it straight and level.

By mid 1943 many American servicemen were stationed in various parts of the country and there was one base near to Stafford. A demonstration of their game of Baseball (Rounders to us) was arranged for one Sunday in the local park in the town. We all attended as a crew, our Canadian members explaining the rules of the game to us (the rules being similar to their Softball). A pleasant afternoon was enjoyed by all. With the course completed we were given leave and orders to report to 1660 Heavy Conversion Unit at Swinderby near Lincoln in seven days time.

Pete Kearsey was on leave at the same time and at a local hostelry we met another member of the RAF, F/Sgt Kent who worked at the Maintenance Unit at RAF Debden. We were invited to his home and met his family, including his daughter Freda (but called Peggy) who had been in another class at school. We spent some time together during the leave.

I also saw Doreen a couple of times and one evening we were going to visit a local cinema. Whilst she was getting ready upstairs I was chatting in the hallway with a priest who, as a friend of the family, had just dropped in. He asked where we were going... when I told him he immediately handed me five shillings (enough for two seats and a drink after). In his deep Irish brogue he said, “Let me treat you both.” Doreen, who was just coming down the stairs, on hearing this leaned down and gave him a big kiss on his cheek leaving a bright red image of her lips. As he wiped it off I was surprised to hear him murmur, “Bloody lipstick.”

Wimpeys at Hixon. The second from the front is BT-T in which we flew an ‘Air Firing’ exercise on 16th August ‘43.

F/O John Young Pilot RCAF

P/O Jack Scott Navigator RCAF

F/Sgt Ted Cachart Wop/Ag *F/Sgt Alan Vidow F/E*
Sgt Len Crossman Gunner *F/Sgt Alan 'Spud' Mahony Gunner*
Photo taken in London, 1945, after return from POW camps

11

No 1660 HEAVY CONVERSION UNIT RAF SWINDERBY

By my eighteenth birthday in June 1943 I had been training for twenty-one months (although I did not consider the four months on the Tow Target flight to be training, it was more like a paid holiday). I had clocked up just over a hundred flying hours on six different aircraft types, with almost two-hundred hours by the 17th August when we completed the O.T.U. course.

At the end of the leave our crew was posted to RAF Lindholme by mistake and after three days, on **13th*** September 1943, we were re-posted to RAF Swinderby in Lincolnshire. (At Lindholm I met up with Bill Cooper, the son of Cyril Cooper who employed me at the bakery).

At HCU we were to convert onto four engined aircraft. On arrival we were all pleased to see some of the crews with whom we had been training at the OTU, including all the 'Musketeers' crews.

At Swinderby we would become a seven man crew by adding a flight engineer and mid upper gunner.

'My' crew:-

Flight Engineer	646931	F/Sgt	AW	Vidow	RAF
M/U Gunner	1602967	Sgt	J	Sykes	RAF

Tom's crew:-

Flight Engineer	1480159	Sgt	E	Calloway	RAF
M/U Gunner	1116830	Sgt	C	Johnson	RAF

Bill's Crew

Flight Engineer	1157645	Sgt	TH	Lee	RAF
M/U Gunner	1087197	F/Sgt	JN	Manuel	RAF

Jimmy's Crew:-

Flight Engineer	185059	Sgt	KR	Marriott	RAF
M/U Gunner	1803629	Sgt	A	Ferguson	RAF

The aircraft were mainly Lancasters with a few Halifaxes and Stirlings. The Lancasters were equipped with the new H2S Radar Navigation Aid and each of these aircraft had an armed guard at night (and possibly during the day as well).

Swinderby was a pre-war permanent station with the conventional 'H' type two storey accommodation blocks. We had central heating with adequate hot baths and showers on each floor, sheer luxury after all the metal or wooden Nissen huts that we had lived in since leaving Blackpool. The accommodation was large dormitory style rooms. Excellent facilities included a gym and a proper mess with a lounge, a snooker room etc.

The NCO's in the 'Musketeers' crews moved into one of the blocks and commandeered almost the entire space in a room on the second floor. On my bedside locker was a framed colour photograph of the chestnut haired Doreen that was greatly admired by all.

However, more memorable to anyone who used the lounge were the really excellent hand painted full sized reproductions of Alberto Vargas' extremely exotic 'Vargas Girls' on each of the wall panels between the waist to ceiling height tall windows.

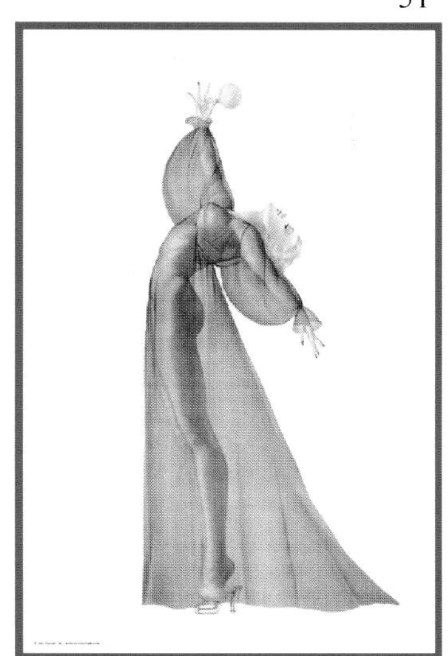

Who I wonder was the artist that painted these Swinderby beauties. … does anybody know?

After we started night flying, if we got to bed at a reasonable time we would still get up for breakfast and then have the best part of the day to do what we liked. We might go to the gym, play snooker, or just lay around on our beds talking, writing letters or reading. One day, a few of us were lying on our beds just reading and chatting. Both of Jimmy's gunners were sound asleep on their beds, but were separated by another bed between theirs. We suddenly all quietened down as we listened to one of them talking in his sleep - to our amazement the other gunner also spoke as if to reply... this continued for quite a few minutes. Although I don't recall what was said, I know we all found it a bit eerie.

We did two trips in a Halifax before changing onto 'The Dream Machine' we had been hoping for - **The Lancaster**. On the 20th September, with screen pilot F/O Buttoner we took off for the first time in this huge powerful aircraft with the roar of those four distinctive sounding engines throbbing through our bodies as it gracefully climbed up into the air... where it belonged. It was every bit as exciting as we had imagined and I admit that **I fell in love - and still am!**

There was also at least one Short Stirling aircraft for training but we never flew in it. The height of it alone made you think about filling in your logbook if you only got in it to have a look around. Some claimed the cockpit canopy was high enough to be above fog or even low cloud whilst the wheels were still on the runway.

Part of our training here was learning the escape routine from a Lancaster for both abandoning by parachute and ditching at sea. We were required to do something like two hours of these drills in a static fuselage by the main hangar, but we practiced a lot more. The friendly rivalry between our crews developed into a challenge to see which crew could do it the fastest. This was soon thrown open to all crews and it was quite usual during any free period to see two or three crews practising with an 'Umpire' armed with stop watch and a referee with a starter's whistle, timing each other. The procedure became automatic resulting in us doing far more training than required.

Later in the story you will appreciate the significance of this.

The routine for abandoning the Lancaster by parachute was:-

The flight engineer, bomb aimer, navigator and pilot would leave by the front hatch in the floor of the bomb aimer's position. The hatch in the floor being removed and dropped through the hole by whoever was nearest.

The wireless operator would take his parachute from the storage rack, climb over the main spar, open the metal door and make his way down the darkened fuselage, check that the mid upper gunner was out of his turret and then proceed to the rear to assist the rear gunner out of his turret (difficult for the gunner due to the bulky clothing he wore). Meanwhile the mid upper gunner would open and fasten back the rear door.

The wireless operator would then be first to sit on the exit step, facing forward in a crouched position and roll out to be followed by the gunners. This lessened the chance of hitting the tail plane, or if you did, it would be your back that struck it and you may still be able to open your 'chute'. The only training we had on using a parachute were verbal instructions on counting to ten before pulling the rip cord handle and how to stop the chute from oscillating and spilling air. Reach up above your head, grasp a strap in each hand and pull downwards to counteract your swing, similar to the way one pulled the ropes of a garden swing but in the opposite direction to stop the 'swing' rather than increase it.

Another tip was to keep one's legs together on landing or else it could be very painful if one straddled a fence.

Dinghy Drill was very similar with the exception that we did it out on a grass area of the airfield where the crew would all sit in a large dinghy. I, and other members of the crew, fired a rocket propelled kite into the air with an aerial wire attached for the dinghy radio.

Dinghy Radio

We were only allowed three attempts and on each try the kite opened but just fell to the ground. An aerial with one end in the sea does not radiate a good enough signal.

The dinghy radio was waterproof and shaped so that it could be held securely between one's thighs. You then turned a handle at a controlled speed so that it generated power and sent out S.O.S. automatically. We had learned how to turn a dinghy the right way up and how to climb into it, in the public swimming baths, whilst at the OTU.

We did 16 training trips, two on Halifaxs and 14 on Lancs - total flying time on this course 17:20 day and 14:40 night. We were now a fully trained Lancaster crew of seven and going on leave... I invited the two Canadians, Johnny and Scotty to come to my home which they accepted.

On leave we did some of the obvious things like popping up to London to a show etc. One evening my father was talking to the skipper whilst looking through my flying log book. He saw some entries 'Fighter affiliation' and 'High level bombing' and assumed we had already been on operations. Showing his concern he asked Johnny all about it. John quickly explained that it was only training and I noticed his relief. As a result of this, and because I had no doubts about us surviving, I did not tell any of my family when we did get onto operations.

I felt that not knowing would be less stressful as they would not have the constant worry when hearing of nightly losses on the radio and wondering if I was one of them.

Another evening, Johnny, Scotty and I went to the Whittington Hotel situated between Rayners Lane and Pinner. There were a number of this type of public house in the area, called hotels, but they were really public houses with a dance hall and bar attached and with extended drinking hours.

The one hour extension from 10-30 to 11-30 made these very popular. We sat at a table in the lounge quietly enjoying a drink and chatting. Over our heads was a ceiling loudspeaker from which (we thought) piped music was being played. Time passed quickly and it was soon 'Last orders please'. I suggested that we should finish our drinks and go round to the ballroom where the bar was still open. Just as we drained our glasses, another tune emanated from the speaker with a girl's voice singing a popular song of that time,

'Coming In On A Wing And A Prayer.'

We walked round the corner and in through the double swing doors of the ballroom. The floor between us and the stage was clear with tables on either side. On the stage, a four piece band was playing 'Coming In On a Wing And A Prayer' and lo and behold, Doreen was the singer. When she saw us come in she squealed with delight, jumped off the stage, ran up and threw her arms around me with a big welcoming kiss. The room was fairly crowded and to our embarrassment there was some applause and smiles as we walked across the dance floor towards a table by the stage where we joined Doreen's mother. It was almost like a scene from some war movie. A party developed and it was after midnight when we all walked home. We said good night to her mother as Doreen was coming with us as we intended to party some more. My father telephoned Peggy and despite the late hour she cycled over to join us. Much later, when we were ready to retire, Doreen and Peggy decided that they would stay the night sharing what was 'my' room and I would sleep on the settee downstairs. They both phoned home, Peggy borrowed a pair of my pyjamas and Doreen was handed a pair of new ones that the skipper had bought whilst on this leave. We all retired and all I recall of the following morning was the skipper's wry comment when Doreen returned the pyjamas, smiling he said,

"I don't think I will be washing these for some time."

Sadly leave was soon over and Johnny, Scotty and I bade farewell to Peggy, Doreen and my parents and departed with our full kit for the train to Lincoln where we then got RAF transport to take us to our new posting.

AIRCREW POSTINGS - 49 SQUADRON FISKERTON OCTOBER 1943

Date	
5th	F/Sgt Roantree RAAF & crew IN from 1660 HCU Swinderby- TE
6th	F/Lt Carfoot & crew IN from 1654 HCU Wigsley- FTR
7th	P/O Wares & crew posted Missing Without Trace- FTR
8th	S/Ldr Miller RNZAF & crew IN from 44 Squadron- TE
12th	F/O Palmer & crew IN from 1654 HCU- FTR
12th	F/Lt Tancred & crew IN from 1654 HCU- FTR
13th	P/O Young RCAF, P/O Scott RCAF, P/O Orchard, Sgt Vidow, Sgt Cachart, Sgt Crossman, Sgt Sykes IN from 1660 HCU- FTR
22nd	F/Sgt Hodgkinson & crew posted Missing Without Trace- FTR
	P/O Tavener & crew posted Missing Without Trace- FTR
	P/O Ratcliffe & crew IN from 1654 HCU -FTR
	P/O Teager & crew IN from 1654 HCU. P/O Teager as '2nd dickie- P.o.W.
24th	P/O Simpson & crew IN from 1654 HCU- TE
26th	F/Lt Pike & crew OUT to 207 Squadron where they failed to return- FTR
29th	F/O Bailey & crew IN from 1660 HCU. F/O Bailey as '2nd dickie'- KIA
29th	F/O Bacon & crew IN from 1660 HCU- FTR

Key: FTR - Failed To Return. TE - Tour Expired (completed). KIA - Killed In Action. 2nd dickie - New pilot under instruction.

Of the 92 men in these crews, 7 were posted out to 207 Sqdn where they FTR. Of the remaining 85, 45 were killed, 19 became PoWs and 21 completed their tours - an attrition rate of over 75%.

12

No 49 SQUADRON
RAF FISKERTON

It was on Wednesday October **13th*** 1943 that we arrived and linked up with the rest of the crew having achieved our objective in becoming members of 49 Squadron, a front line bomber squadron in 5 Group. The base was a wartime airfield built between the villages of Fiskerton and Reepham, about 5 miles east of Lincoln City. Its main runway running east to west pointed straight at the Cathedral. The base callsign was 'Passout' and the aircraft 'Bandlaw'. Parts of Fiskerton village were within the camp boundaries and walking along the roadway from the NCOs' and Officers' messes you passed two pubs before you got to the WAAF's quarters. (Not that we ever ventured as far as that !)

We had a few days familiarisation and getting settled in. Then, on the 18th October we did a Night Flying Test (NFT) on an operational Lancaster for the crew that would be taking it on operations that night. We could not do this at Fiskerton as the main runway was unusable due to the concrete crumbling in a number of places. In order that the squadron could continue operating the aircraft and ground staff were moved over to nearby Dunholme Lodge whilst the aircrew stayed at Fiskerton, being ferried to Dunholme and back by crew bus or lorry.

We donned our flying clothing, took our parachutes and harnesses and climbed aboard a Dodge tilt truck and drove right through the centre of Lincoln, waving out of the back of the truck to the folks in the streets on our way to Dunholme. The NFT on EA-A (ED999) completed, we handed the aircraft over to the ground staff to get it fuelled and bombed up ready for the crew to take it to Hanover.

Fiskerton Airfield - note the main runway that to the west points straight at the three towers of Lincoln Cathedral.

We were ferried back the same way, not exactly publicising that operations were on that night, but pretty obvious to those who knew the routine. We did a similar NFT the next day on EA-N (JB231) which was planned to attack Augsburg but the operation was cancelled. Over the next two weeks we did Radar training and five more NFT's but these were flown from Fiskerton which still had one of the shorter runways functional. When not flying, time was spent in many ways. Physical exercise was obtained by chopping logs with felling axes for the mess fires, or on cycles (if we could find one) getting to know the area or even exercising our arm muscles by tasting the odd glass of local brew, purely in the interests of research of course.

Much to my surprise, Musketeer Jimmy and his crew were posted in to 49 Squadron at the end of October. His skipper, F/O Bailey went as a 2nd Dickie (new pilot with experienced crew) to Dusseldorf with F/O Cottingham on November 3rd. Then he took his own crew to Modane on 11th November and then did another 2nd Dickie operation with Cottingham when all eight members of the crew perished.

Jimmy and crew, now without a pilot, were posted back to 1660 HCU at Swinderby. There they crewed up with ex-49er pilot, F/Lt Ted Tickler who had won the CGM for bringing back his badly damaged Lancaster whilst wounded following a mine laying operation on 27th February 1943. Now fully recovered from his injuries and after short courses at Swinderby and Syerston, the 'new' Tickler crew were posted to 57 Squadron at East Kirkby.

As our crew continued on its pre-operational build up, 49 Squadron and Bomber Command continued to take the war to the enemy's heartland. After nine days without operating, on the 18th October W/Cmdr Adams led 14 of the unit's Lancasters away from Dunholme bound for Hanover.

The force of 360 Lancasters found the target cloud covered which made marking difficult for the Pathfinders; unfortunately 18 aircraft failed to return but all 49's bombed without any hitches and returned safely.

The weather on Wednesday 20th October was appalling yet around tea time the aircrews once again climbed on the crew buses for their trip over to Dunholme and Fiskerton became a ghost town for the evening. The squadron sent 15 Lancs to Leipzig and all returned safely.

On Friday 22nd October, ops were again posted at Flights and yet again our crew were not listed. The boys were briefed for Kassel with 11 aircraft from the unit taking part. Next morning we learned that two of the squadron's crews had failed to return, F/S Hodgkinson and crew in O-Oboe (JB416) and P/O Taverner and crew in P-Peter (JB413).

FTR JB416	F/S	A.	Hodgkinson	Pilot	(Killed)
(EA-O)	Sgt	R.E.	Harnett	F/E	(Killed)
'B Flt'	Sgt	A.G.	Fisher	NAV	(Killed)
	F/S	J.	Foley	W/AG	(Killed)
	Sgt	D.	Durrell RCAF	A/G	(Killed)
Crew on their	Sgt	R.A.	Ford	B/A	(Killed)
11th operation	Sgt	R.F.	Ricketts	A/G	(Killed)
FTR JB413	P/O	P.A.	Taverner	Pilot	(Killed)
(EA-P)	Sgt	W.	Kemp	F/E	(P.o.W.)
'B Flt'	Sgt	I.	Spence	NAV	(P.o.W.)
	Sgt	R.H.	Norman	W/AG	(P.o.W.)
	Sgt	N.C.	Dunbabin	A/G	(P.o.W.)
Crew on their	Sgt	R.K.	Drinnan RCAF	B/A	(P.o.W.)
3rd operation	F/S	E.E.	Parker RAAF	A/G	(Killed)

These were both from 'B' Flight. - our Flight. This was the last op. to be flown from Dunholme Lodge by 49 Squadron as Fiskerton's main runway reopened on the 24th October.

'FIDO'

Whilst operations were being carried out from Dunholme Lodge, secret experiments had been carried out at Fiskerton. As the long winter nights approached they brought along adverse weather with the inevitable fog – but the Air Ministry were on the case. The 'boffins' had come up with an answer to the problem which they entitled 'Fog Investigation Dispersal Operation' or FIDO for short.

This unique but basic system involved pumping petrol mixed with alcohol along pipes installed down both sides of the main runway. When ignited, huge flames shot into the sky where the resultant heat created a thermal effect, which in turn lifted the fog away from the runway. Fiskerton was one of the first three airfields in England to try out this dramatic invention. The system would come to our crew's assistance on more than one occasion during our operational period.

When the first tests of this system were made rumours of burning aircraft and/or buildings abounded in the villages of Reepham and Fiskerton.

2/3rd November, 1943;DUSSELDORF

"Operational at last!"

Our pre-op training had continued on the squadron with various cross country flights and H2S radar practice. Bomber Command had been thwarted by the weather for several days with no operational flying able to take place. With some improvement promised for that night the tele-printers from

Fiskerton FIDO - photograph taken in daylight

Group rattled into action. Nearly 600 bombers were required for an attack against the German city of Dusseldorf and our crew appeared on 49 Squadron's Order of Battle.

The culmination of two years hard training was now about to come to fruition.

We were allotted Lancaster U-Uncle (JB473) and later that morning we took the aircraft up for the most diligent Night Flying Test. We then tried to get some rest, impossible to sleep - adrenalin pumping - excitement building - clock ticking slowly. Eventually it was time to have our pre-operational evening meal and then to briefing.

Each individual 'trade' had separate briefings - for example, wop/ag's would be briefed by the Wireless Leader, gunners by the Gunnery Leader etc. Then, as a full crew we would attend the main briefing where we would receive weather reports, bomb loads, heights and courses to fly and the target.

Tonight's target was Dusseldorf in the Ruhr, or 'Happy Valley' as it was known by bomber crews. After donning our flying kit we stood outside the locker room waiting for transport out to the waiting bombers. Our crew bus came and we piled in with other crews and set off around the peri-track to 'B' Flight's dispersal area on the northern side of the airfield.

At our dispersal the WAAF driver announced, **"U–Uncle."**

With pre-flight checks completed and engines run-up to temperature we taxied out to join the rest of the squadron waddling round to the main runway. One by one the Lancasters received the green light from the control caravan which sent them hurtling down the concrete strip to climb slowly but surely into the night air.

Our turn - Johnny turned 'Uncle' onto the threshold - a flash of green, vivid in the fading light. Johnny with a quick thumbs up and calm, "Here we go boys", released the brakes which let out a sharp hiss. 'U-Uncle' was out of the blocks. From the astrodome I acknowledged the waves from the small knot of squadron well-wishers by the caravan.

I then looked ahead to the west and the string of runway lights rapidly rushing towards me. There, just discernable on the horizon in last light stood the three towers of Lincoln Cathedral. Time of take-off 17.05hrs.

We were part of a force of almost 600 bombers of which 49 Squadron contributed 18. The operation was memorable for the fact that we were confronting the enemy for the first time. As a very immature 18 year old youth, to me all flying was just fun and each and every incident an exciting adventure. At no time during flying training or on operations did I ever consider the possibility of being killed or injured. It might happen to others but the simple logic of youthful immaturity is:... **'It won't happen to me'.**

With helmet on and my headset plugged into the radio, listening for any instructions that might be sent out, I would stand with my head in the astrodome (just above my crew position) absorbing what was happening around me.

During an operation, 5 Group HQ would broadcast every half an hour and these would be recorded in the log by the wop/ag and passed to the pilot or navigator - there might be a recall or change of target etc. Between taking these messages it was more important to be another pair of eyes in the astrodome rather than just sitting at the radio.

On approaching the target it was so thrilling to see the flak with tracers and searchlights hosing across the sky, seeing the fires burning below and the explosions from the bombs dropped by the aircraft who were ahead of us, then flying right over the target and the sudden 'lift' of the aeroplane as our bombs were released.

It was awesome, exciting and I have to say that I never gave a thought to what damage the bombs were doing - it was war and I was part of it.

On reflection, I guess that in some ways we felt secure within the cocoon of the enclosed metal fuselage and what we saw outside was like seeing it on a film screen - whatever, I would not have missed it for 'all the tea in China and India as well'.

We landed safely back at Fiskerton at exactly 22.00hrs. The ground crew met us at dispersal and congratulated us with hand shakes all round - a job well done, at last we were operational.

The journey by crew bus round to the ops block for de-brief interrogation was one of quiet reflection, each of us deep in our own thoughts.

We entered a busy smoke filled ops room to be given a most welcome cocoa laced with rum. The crew assembled round a trestle table to be interrogated by a smiling WAAF Intelligence Officer.

Johnny gave her most of the 'gen' with other members of the crew adding their info; "*Arrived over Dusseldorf at 19.54hrs at 21,000ft - no cloud but plenty of smoke and haze. Bomb aimer had one green Target Indicator in his sights - we did not see our own bombs explode. Attack was fairly concentrated and the met forecast was accurate. Gee was u/s and 72 bundles of Window were dropped. Defences not up to Ruhr standards.*" (Gee - radar positioning device.)

(That final statement is worthy of the 'line book' coming from a 'sprog crew'). "Thank you Gentlemen, enjoy your sleep", and off we trundled. But through bleary eyes it was noticed that the ops board showed two crews overdue.

At breakfast after a good night's rest we learned that the squadron had indeed lost two crews from the Dusseldorf trip. F/Lt Thomas and crew in R-Roger were on their 20th operation - a night fighter got them. Three crew members escaped by parachute before the Lanc exploded near Cologne.

The second missing aircraft was piloted by F/Lt Carfoot. On this their second operation, the crew of E-Easy were set on fire by flak and then attacked by a JU88.

The pilot held onto his blazing bomber enabling three crew members to escape before the aircraft disintegrated in a massive explosion killing F/Lt Carfoot and the remainder of the crew.

FTR ED438	F/L	C.G.	Thomas	Pilot	(Killed)
(EA-R)	P/O	J.E.	Teager	2ndPilot	(P.o.W.)
'B Flt'	Sgt	N.D.	Panter	F/E	(P.o.W.)
	F/S	W.G	Clutterbuck	NAV	(Killed)
	Sgt	W.A.	Payne	W/AG	(P.o.W.)
	Sgt	H.	Minns	A/G	(Killed)
Crew on their	F/O	C.P.	Ross	B/A	(Killed)
20th operation	Sgt	G.E.	Boxer	A/G	(Killed)

FTR JB305	F/L	N.H.	Carfoot	Pilot	(Killed)
(EA-E)	Sgt	J.S.	Mason	F/E	(Killed)
'A Flt'	Sgt	H.D.	Church	NAV	(P.o.W.)
	Sgt	H.L.	Wood	W/AG	(Killed)
	Sgt	W.H.	Marson	A/G	(Killed)
Crew on their	F/S	S.G.	Putman RCAF	B/A	(P.o.W.
2nd operation	F/S	S.M.	List RAAF	A/G	(Killed)

We also learned later that Sykes, our mid upper gunner, who was living in another hut, had sat on his bed and declared that he was not going to fly on operations again. He had disappeared from the station before we heard of this and we believe that he had been classified LMF (Lack of moral fibre) and posted away.

This was a drastic but essential measure as it could have been demoralising if one could 'back out' of operational duties. A question of a 'bad apple' affecting the whole barrel.

During November we did a number of tests on a new Lancaster but the question about this remains unanswered as there does not appear to be any specific record of what and why we were doing those tests. I do recall doing some very low daylight flying over the North Sea and Lincolnshire countryside, probably to the annoyance of many of the farmers and locals. I also remember one of the aircraft being taken into the hanger and being examined by a number of civilians and RAF personnel.

On Wednesday evening, 10th November, sixteen of the squadron's Lancasters edged their way around Fiskerton's darkened peri-track. They were bound for Modane in Southern France to attack a railway target. Five aircraft had already taken off when W/O Webb and crew in P-Peter began their run. Shortly after tail-up, the port tyre burst lurching JB533 into a massive ground loop. When the bomber eventually came to rest the crew made a rapid evacuation as the aircraft caught fire.

This quickly became an inferno. The fire crews decided their task was becoming hopeless and a tactical withdrawal was made. The bomb load eventually exploded scattering fragments of the Lancaster for miles.

In mid November there was a Sergeants' Mess Dance, our crew were all there, the three officers having been invited by us NCOs. I saw Dot Everette, the MT driver who drove one of the crew buses, talking to a young lady who was wearing a small brooch in the shape of an Air Gunner brevet - this was identical to one that I had recently bought in Lincoln for Doreen's birthday that was on the 4th November.

I went over and Dot introduced me. Her name was Betty Wilcox and she told me she lived in Reepham, just at the back of the airfield.

During the conversation Betty asked which was my aircraft - security was not a problem as all the aircraft could be seen by both Reepham and Fiskerton residents, and as Dot knew her personally I felt no need to be over cautious. When I told her it was N-Nan, she said, "Would you ask your pilot to park the aircraft sideways at the dispersal - when he runs up the engines it blows dirt all over the washing?" The request was passed on and the aircraft position duly adjusted resulting in her mother, Mrs Wilcox, adopting the crew and inviting any, or all of us to pop round any time we were free. I still remember the fresh ham and brown bread sandwiches (possibly home made bread). Folks in the countryside did not suffer too much from food rationing.

Betty Wilcox

I am sure that this was the night that someone 'spiked' Dot's drink, she was singing along with the rest of us gathered round the piano when she suddenly passed out. Three of the crew and I picked her up, one holding each corner, and carried her all the way back to the WAAF's quarters. Once there we walked straight into her hut which was STRICTLY OUT OF BOUNDS. We ascertained which was Dot's bed from one of the partially dressed young ladies, laid her gently on it and with broad smiles all round, we bade these giggling fair maidens goodnight and walked back to our mess.

The Ferry Boat

There were times when it was good to get away from the mess and a very popular 'local' pub that usually had someone playing the 'Joanna' was the Ferry Boat on the other side of the River Witham. It was also a good opportunity for air crew and ground staff to get together socially, which helped improve the relationship.

Fiskerton's Five Mile House and Windlass Chain Ferry over the River Witham to the railway station. Illustration by John Ward and copied from his book on 49 Squadron, Beware Of The Dog At War. (JoTe Publications)

It was a very long walk to get there if you went by the normal roads and lanes.

A much quicker way was only a short walk down a footpath from the camp to the 'Chain Ferry' at Five Mile House. This was also a short cut to the railway station. The ferry consisted of an unmanned floating raft with a continuous chain loop that went round a wheel mounted on each bank and through metal rings on one of the side rails.

You just reached forward and pulled the chain and the raft floated across. It was quite common for revellers returning this way to rock the raft from side to side.

It was later learned that one night in the previous September, the ferry had turned over and two ground staff were unfortunately drowned.

Although we were all young, fit and full of 'spirit', I would not like to give you the impression that we drank a lot - but we did tend to live for today and let tomorrow look after itself, and in our 'off duty' time did the best we could to enjoy ourselves.

It is amazing what one's brain stores away to suddenly reappear as clear as day….. some little incident that had no real significance at the time. One such recollection popped into my memory whilst writing this story, one that I had not recalled since it happened.

A rather foggy day, we were not flying but I was out on the airfield with a few others when a small aircraft came in and landed.

It was an American fighter plane that was lost and dropped in to ask control where he was. That was the explanation we were given, and knowing the Yanks, quite plausible.

13

BATTLE OF BERLIN

With the longer dark nights, Bomber Command could now mount a series of concentrated attacks against the 'Big City', Berlin. This onslaught, which would consist of 16 major raids over four months, would later become known as the 'Battle of Berlin'. On Thursday 18th November, 'Bomber' Harris ordered 440 aircraft to attack the city - 49 Squadron put up 19 Lancasters led by W/Cmdr Adams in O-Oboe. All 49's aircraft returned from the operation, with eight landing away from base. C-Charlie (JB235) landed back at Fiskerton with the squadron's only casualty - during the return flight a young Canadian rear gunner's life slipped away through lack of oxygen.

The Berlin battle continued on 22nd November when over 760 bombers attacked the German capital. The squadron sent 16 aircraft of which F/O Cottingham and crew in G-George (JB368) failed to return. (As mentioned earlier, on board was F/O Bailey - Jimmy Goddard's original pilot.)

With little rest, crews were back to Berlin on the next night, 23rd November. The squadron sent 14 aircraft and yet again our crew did not appear on the Battle Order. All 49's aircraft returned safely with the exception of F/O Turner and crew in S-Sugar (JB229).

Descending through low cloud to determine landfall and with 1,000ft showing on the altimeter, the pilot was shocked to hit the sea! The Lanc careered up the beach coming to rest in the shallow water at Chapel-St Leonards on the Lincolnshire coast. All the crew were safe if not a little shaken, but they soon recovered and returned to the squadron.

Crashes were inevitable and the following drastic incident is just one example. 'Funnel' describes the imaginary area on the approach to the runway, shaped like a funnel, into which the aircraft turns and lines up with the runway.

26/27th November 1943

Extract from 'Beware Of The Dog At War'.

(see bibliography)

At 01.02hrs. Sgt Roy Richardson RAAF (JB235) flying 'Bandlaw C-Charlie' entered the 'funnel'. Next in the stack behind C-Charlie was 'Bandlaw A-Able' flown by fellow Australian, F/Sgt Clive Roantree (JB466).

The following extract is from Clive's own book, "To Fly Lancasters", and is reproduced here with his kind permission.

"*We positioned ourselves to land immediately after C-Charlie. He would turn into the funnel, whilst we were on the down-wind leg and should be clear of the runway as we touched down.*

The two parallel bars of fire, one on either side of the runway could be clearly seen with bars of flame at each end to stop the fog rolling into the cleared area. On our practice (November 3rd), we had found that after we turned into the funnel at 600 feet and lined up with the runway, as we approached, the fire on the cross bar reflected on the perspex windshield so that it was impossible for the pilot to see out.

To offset the problem my flight engineer called height and airspeed as soon as we lined up on the runway at 600ft. For the inexperienced pilot it could be a frightening experience as it is not until the aircraft crossed the bar of flame at less than 100 feet that it was possible to see clearly and then make a visual landing. Subsequently a shield was placed in front of the bar of flame to prevent windscreen reflection.

On this night, with wheels down, pitch in fully fine with 20 degrees of flap, we were at the end of the down-wind leg ready to make our turn across wind before entering the funnel, when there was a dull flash on the ground right at the beginning of the funnel. I knew that an aircraft had crashed and to my horror realised that it must be Richardson in C-Charlie.

I continued the landing procedure turning across wind and there, right below us was an aircraft on fire! Giving the crew the order that we were going to overshoot, I called flying control, 'Hello Passout, Bandlaw Able over shooting - an aircraft has crashed and is on fire in the funnel - I say again an aircraft has crashed and is on fire in the funnel'.

There was a short pause before we were called again from flying control to repeat the message. Because of the flames from FIDO and the position of the control tower, they could not see the burning aircraft. After completing our overshoot procedure we continued around the circuit and this time as we were completing the downwind leg, there was a flash of flame on the ground as C-Charlie's fuel tanks exploded.

Nerves and senses were now tuned to the dangers as we carefully made our approach in copybook style. There was a slight lift as we crossed the heat rising from the bar at the beginning of the runway and A-Able set down smoothly in a three-point-landing. It was bad enough when crews were missing over enemy territory, but there was an awful accentuation of loss when a crew had completed its mission and disaster struck so close to home and safety."

Tragically, the Lancaster burning in the funnel was that of the Richardson crew, returning from their first operation. Sgt Allan 'Spud' Mahony, the Lancaster's top turret gunner described what happened on that fateful night, during an interview with the author in 1991.

"We descended into fog as we approached the glare of Fiskerton's FIDO runway. Suddenly, without warning, I felt the Lancaster's undercarriage touch down... we were still a good way out from the runway so we must have landed on farmland. Seconds later there was an almighty impact and I banged my forehead hard... clambering down from the turret in a dazed state, I at first made for the door, then I realised the kite had broken apart so I exited through the break. I staggered round to the rear turret and banged on the perspex, but could get no response; returning to the front section, I was confronted by flames everywhere."

Author's note: The Lancaster had hit a drainage ditch with its main wheels and the impact had broken the fuselage just aft of the wing. Spud's only thoughts were to help the rest of his crew and without hesitation this tough Aussie gunner re-entered the fiercely burning aircraft. Allan continues with his painful memories:

"The cockpit was a sheet of flame, but I could just make out the skipper still in his seat... I went forward and could see his clothing was on fire... grabbing him by his parachute harness I pulled like hell, but the harness had been burnt part through and it gave way sending me tumbling back into the radio compartment. Regaining my feet, I went back into the heat again to try to get Roy out, but a stronger force seemed to be pulling me back; I then became aware of two figures holding me and one was shouting 'it's too late mate, it's too late... nothing can be done now'. The next thing I remember was being taken to the sick bay."

Sgt Mahony had in fact been restrained and then rescued from his heroic deeds by the station's firemen. The crash crews also recovered the unconscious rear gunner, Colin Winterborn; he had only been on the squadron a few days having been IN with the 'freshmen' Simpson crew, with whom he went on to survive a successful tour. Sadly the remaining five crew members all perished in the crash.

The gloomy evening's tragedies had not yet come to an end; W/O Ron Brunt (JB362) had failed to return from Berlin. The 21 year old pilot and his crew, flying in D-Dog, were brought down over Berlin and only the bomb aimer, Sgt Burrows, managed to escape with his life; their navigator, Sgt Fred Ashman was only 19 years of age.

FTR JB362	W/O	R.	Brunt	Pilot	(Killed)
(EA-D)	Sgt	H.	Bronsky	F/E	(Killed)
'A Flt'	Sgt	F.E.	Ashman	NAV	(Killed)
	Sgt	R. W.	Norley DFM	W/AG	(Killed)
Crew on their	F/S	R.P.	O'Dea	A/G	(Killed)
13th operation	Sgt	J.G.	Burrows	B/A	(P.o.W)
	Sgt	E.D.	Wilson	A/G	(Killed)
Crashed	Sgt	R.J.	Richardson RAAF	Pilot	(Killed)
JB235	Sgt	H.G.	Boswell	F/E	(Killed)
(EA-C) '	Sgt	H.	Carr	NAV/B	(Killed)
A Flt'	Sgt	L.H.	Cartwright	W/AG	(Killed)
	Sgt	M.O.	Mahoney RAAF	A./G	(Injured)
Crew on their	P/O	H.	Lowe (USA) RCAF	B/A	(Killed)
1st operation	Sgt	C.	Winterborn	A/G	(Injured)

Around the same time as the Richardson crash, and unbeknown to Fiskerton control, the crew of a severely damaged Lancaster Mk II from 408 RCAF Squadron, also returning from Berlin, was making a desperate attempt to find Fiskerton's FIDO sanctuary. Their struggle ended abruptly when the pilot was forced to land in open country. With extreme skill born out of desperation to survive, the pilot brought the aircraft down in fields near the sewage works alongside the Lincoln to Washingborough road. Miraculously, on this fog-bound night all the crew walked away unharmed.

2/3rd December, 1943; BERLIN

Thursday 2nd December saw a continuation of the bombing attacks on Berlin. Despite high wind forecasts both at base and over Germany, 450 plus bombers set out for the 'Big City and by 16.45hrs Fiskerton had dispatched 14 Lancasters. Bombing was scattered owing to the incorrect forecasts but some industrial areas were hit. As well as strong winds the bomber force also had to contend with numerous fighters. The German controllers had predicted Berlin as the target well in advance of the bomber's arrival and as a result a total of 40 bombers with their crews were lost.

It was our second operation and our first to the 'Big City'. Still being one man short we took a 'spare gunner', a Canadian R159175 Sgt E R Caldwell. Our allotted Lancaster was again U-Uncle (JB473). We departed Fiskerton at 16.36hrs. and carried out, for us, an uneventful operation, with nothing specific to record or even remember, but on our return, base was shrouded in fog. Visibility was down to less than 800yds, with low radiation fog no more than 100ft deep. Shortly before 23.00hrs the order had been given to ignite the FIDO burners. We arrived back over the coast just before midnight and from many miles away we could see the glow of FIDO through the fog. It was an amazing experience; as usual I had my head in the astrodome and I could see the outline of the runway illuminated through the cloud and fog. The pilot descended into the fog and lined up on the visible strips of flame. We touched down (or should I say 'floated down') perfectly then travelled through those great walls of fire on both sides of the runway; it was just unbelievable.

The usual 'well done' came from the ground crew who were always grateful when 'their charge' was brought back un-scathed and healthy!

At de-brief our crew gave their account of the evening; *"Reached Berlin and bombed 20.22hrs at 23,000ft in 3rd wave. Cloud 7/10ths with tops 1,000ft. Centre of 3 Target Indicators in sights. Thin chain of fires running north to south of target area. Attack not developed to judge results."*

W/O Bob Petty and crew from 49 Squadron failed to return from Berlin. On their way to the target J- Jig's rear gunner, Ed Smith, reported that his guns were u/s, but the crew still decided to press-on. During the bombing run they were attacked by an Me110. Owen Roberts in the top turret managed to hit one of the fighter's engines before one of his guns jammed. Continuing the bomb run Owen spotted another Me110 just below them but when he tried to fire his guns they were either jammed or out of ammunition. To add to their troubles flak then struck the starboard inner engine which burst into flames immediately. Without hesitation, Bob gave the order to bale out. Six members of the crew (including 2nd pilot, Sgt Tucker) survived to become PoWs. Sadly the bomb aimer, Bill Walke was killed along with the rear gunner Ed Smith, who although seen to bale out, has no known grave.

FTR JB371	W/O	R.W.	Petty	Pilot	(P.o.W.)
(EA-J)	Sgt	A.	Tucker	2nd Pilot	(P.o.W.)
'A Flt'	Sgt	G.	Lumsden	F/E	(P.o.W.)
	Sgt	T.	Tullock	NAV	(P.o.W.)
	Sgt	S.J.	Richards	W/AG	(P.o.W.)
	Sgt	O.	Roberts	A/G	(P.o.W.)
Crew on their	F/S	W.A.	Walke	B/A	(Killed)
17th operation	Sgt	E.	Smith	A/G	(Missing)

In early December I received a letter from Kathleen Brady, 'Musketeer' Tom's mother, telling me the very sad news that Tom had been reported missing on November 26th and asking if I had any further information about him. Regretfully I had to give a negative answer, we were not privy to such information and Tom was on another squadron. I wrote back saying that I sincerely hoped that we would soon hear that he was a Prisoner of War.

F/Sgt Alan 'Spud' Mahony RAAF Mid Upper Gunner

One night the skipper was waiting at a bus stop in Lincoln and got chatting to an Australian gunner. When he heard that he was one of only two survivors of JB235 that had crashed in the funnel on 2nd December and did not have a crew, he was invited to join ours. This was 'Spud' Mahony, he fitted in well with us and added a bit more to the 'International Flavour'.

16/17th December, 1943; BERLIN

This was our second visit to this target but this time in 'our' Lancaster EA-N (JB231), (nicknamed Nancy Pants by Dot Everette, the MT driver). Bad weather had prevented the bombers operating for almost two weeks and during this time the usual in and out postings had taken place. Amongst the postings 'out' were P/O Vic Edy and crew who were 'tour expired'. For those crews who still had it to do, Thursday night of the 16th saw them back on the road to Berlin once again.

An all Lancaster force of 483 plus PFF Mosquitoes attacked a cloud covered target using sky-markers. No. 49 Squadron had two new crews operating; Canadian F/O Bill Healey (JB679) and crew flying D-Dog, and P/O Gordon Ratcliffe (JB545) and crew in O-Oboe.

Our dispersal was the furthest away on 'B' Flight - the last three were 'P', 'O' and then 'N'. As the crew bus 'whined' its laborious way around the perimeter it eventually grated to a halt and a female voice announced, "O-Oboe." Out bundled the sprog Ratcliffe crew for their first op - we were ships in the night really, the crew being 'new bods' - but we gave them a cheery farewell with the usual;

"Can I have your egg if you don't come back?" etc.....

They didn't come back - less than three hours later their young lives would be ended and their lifeless remains would be strewn across a Dutch polder.

German night fighters had managed to intercept the main force whilst en-route over Holland and it was here that Oberleutnant Heinz Wolfgang Schnaufer, the German night fighter ace, shot down the unsuspecting Ratcliffe crew using the dreaded 'Schrage Musik' (an upward firing canon mounted on the top of the German aircraft's fuselage).

Their Lancaster came down between Oldertrijne and Sonnega where recovery of the bodies proved extremely difficult due to the marshy ground. They are all buried together in Wolvega Cemetery.

"Next stop N-Nan." - "Cheers Dot, thanks for the lift - see you when we get back - don't be late."

Twenty-five Lancasters had been brought down over enemy territory - but the losses did not stop there! Returning over Eastern England, tired crews found low cloud covered many of their bases. From Yorkshire down to Cambridgeshire a further 32 bombers were lost as a result of crashes or being abandoned when their desperate crews baled out.

No. 1 Group, whose airfields were situated on or near the Lincolnshire Wolds, suffered the heaviest - fifteen 1 Group Lancasters with their crews perished on this dreadful night. Bomber Command survivors refer to this tragedy as 'Black Thursday'.

On that night, we returning crews of 49 Squadron (and other 5 Group squadrons) were unaware of the plight and subsequent carnage being suffered by our comrades only miles from our own 'clear' runways.

When returning back over England at night I used to marvel at the number of airfield outer marker lights that could be seen (some overlapping). It was whilst recalling memories for this book that I suddenly remembered this particular night.

As we flew across Eastern England we could see the burning aircraft on the ground glowing through the hazy cloud. Strange, I must have put the tragedy of this night to the back of my mind. Why weren't they diverted to 5 Group airfields that were relatively clear?

We rolled into interrogation just after 1am. As usual Johnny did most of the de-brief; *"Berlin 20.00hrs at 22,000ft in 3rd wave. Green Target Indicators very concentrated but Wanganui flares scattered. Fires not seen owing to weather conditions. Centre of green T.Is. which went down at 20.07hrs in sights".*

On reflection it would appear that we spent seven minutes in the target area!

FTR JB545	P/O	G.L.	Ratcliffe	Pilot	(Killed)
(EA-O)	Sgt	A.E.	Marsland	F/E	(Killed)
'B Flt'	Sgt	E.	Holloway	NAV	(Killed)
	Sgt	W.T.	Rees	W/AG	(Killed)
	F/S	R.	Losa RCAF	A/G	(Killed)
Crew on their	Sgt	W.R.	Day	B/A	(Killed)
1st operation	F/S	B.J.V.	King RAAF	A/G	(Killed)

Just before Christmas I was invited for a meal with the Wilcox family and I happened to mention to Betty that for three nights running I had dreamed about being in a Prisoner of War Camp. She confirms that I had told her that if she looked out of her window one morning and we had not come back, she would know I would be a Prisoner Of War.

Was this foresight? A premonition?
A vision of the future? Or just wishful thinking?

20/21st December, 1943; FRANKFURT

Our fourth operation, once again in EA-N, and once again uneventful for us. Of the 15 aircraft from Fiskerton that set out for Frankfurt, two were new crews piloted by; Sgt Meggison (JB727) in S-Sugar and Sgt Lett (JB399) in H-Harry. German controllers quickly plotted the force of 650 aircraft and night fighters began to take a heavy toll before the bombers were able to reach their target.

A total of 41 aircraft failed to return - 6.3 per cent of those dispatched.

Over the target the Pathfinders had not expected the thick cloud cover which now thwarted their pre-planned ground-marking. Added to this, the Germans lit a decoy fire and were using dummy target indicators. Despite all these setbacks the RAF were able to inflict a good deal of damage to Frankfurt and its outlying townships.

No. 49 Squadron's Lancasters were equipped with H2S radar (one of the first 'main force' squadrons to operate this aid) and this enabled our crews to locate the target better.

We had left Fiskerton in the early evening and after a six hour trip we were back at base before midnight.

"Take-off 17.12hrs. Reached Frankfurt 19.55hrs at 21,000ft—9/10ths low cloud. H2S identification. Considerable amount of short bombing. Bombed centre of group of yellow T.Is. Pathfinders very poor –plenty of fighter flares seen. Successful sortie. Landed 23.19hrs."

P/O Alf Blackmore (JB467), a 21 year old pilot and holder of the DFC, along with his crew, failed to return to Fiskerton and were reported missing, their aircraft crashed near Hanau. The crew lie at rest together in the Durnbach War Cemetery in Germany.

FTR JB467	P/O	A.H	Blackmore DFC	Pilot	(Killed)
(EA-T)	Sgt	T.S.	Daniel	F/E	(Killed)
'B Flt'	P/O	B.J.	Saville	NAV	(Killed)
	Sgt	S.V.	Domleo	W/OP	(Killed)
	Sgt	G.S.	Lawn	A/G	(Killed)
Crew on their	F/S	H.T.	Evans	A/B	(Killed)
15th operation	Sgt	P.W.	Booth	A/G	(Killed)

23/24th December, 1943; BERLIN

Fourteen Lancasters had been detailed for ops but we had to cancel at the last minute due to technical problems - always a galling situation for crews. Everyone gets mentally prepared to go and then the anti climax felt is tremendous. There's no feeling of relief - the ops have got to be completed at some time, so lets get them out of the way!

The remaining thirteen aircraft became airborne during the first hour of Christmas Eve. Berlin was yet again covered by cloud which resulted in the force of 390 bombers making a scattered attack in the south-eastern parts of the city; 15 Lancasters were lost.

All our squadron's crews completed their sorties without trouble although S/Ldr 'Dusty' Miller and crew (JB314) had to bomb 10 minutes late owing to his port inner engine not giving full power.

All of the squadron were safely down at Fiskerton by 08.15hrs. and after de-brief and a welcome breakfast their beds beckoned, but just before they retired to their perishing cold billets news had filtered down from Group that the squadron was 'stood down' for the evening. Tired they may have been, but it was a high-spirited bunch of aircrew that prepared for a good day's sleep whilst contemplating an operational free Christmas Eve. In the meantime, our crew took advantage of a few more hours in bed!

CHRISTMAS EVE 1943

Fortunately the weather prevented any operations being planned for Christmas Eve and it seemed that almost everybody on camp headed into Lincoln. On normal weekends you were lucky if you found a pub that had any beer after about 9 o'clock and Len (the rear gunner) and I decided that it would be a waste of time as Lincoln would be a 'sea of blue uniforms' and the pubs would run dry quite early.

We opted to go to our own mess. On arrival we found it contained two corporals who served behind the bar, the

Station Warrant Officer and a flight sergeant from aircraft maintenance. Len could not drink much beer as it very quickly effected him, but he could sip whisky all evening.

We ordered two whiskies with orange squash - what a mixture! I still do not know where this originated but that is what we drank. I believe that the other four also drank it with us and it all got a little hazy. We played some snooker and put records on the radiogram whilst sipping more of the concoction. About 10.30 the first bus load of revellers returned from Lincoln. They rushed up to the bar as they'd had hardly anything to drink in town. Seeing us standing quietly by the bar sipping our drinks there were remarks like, "Look at these miserable S... 's, give them a drink." Thus our glasses were exchanged for the 'magical kind' that never seemed to be empty no matter how much we drank.

In the fireplace there was an enormous glowing fire generated by a large log which our crew had helped to liberate from the main tree trunk. Len and I were standing by this furnace - not a good idea for Len soon passed out. From this point my mind was a blank until I awoke lying in a field halfway back to the billet, minus my jacket and soaking wet. Some late revellers were walking by and helped me back to my hut. They told me afterwards that when I saw my bed, I said, "That's what I am looking for", climbed in to it fully clothed and went straight to sleep.

In the morning, to my surprise I did not have a hangover but I did have a very badly swollen knee. Dressing and doing the normal ablutions were somewhat difficult but I managed somehow and with two brooms as crutches, I made my way to the mess. Just inside the back door was a metal heated serving counter and as I entered, Margaret, a very nice and friendly WAAF, 'tut-tutted' at me and said, "I have something of yours, wait there." She disappeared into the kitchen and returned holding a wooden spoon with my 'best blue' jacket hanging on the handle caked with mud that had dried hard overnight. She stood it on the counter where it remained standing upright. In the pocket was my wallet that contained quite a few pounds that I had won at cards recently.

I then discovered (from some of the more sober revellers from that night) that when Len passed out I had tried to carry him back to the billet on my shoulder but had tripped over a chair and fallen heavily on one knee. I then apparently hobbled out of the back door where I must have passed out, falling into a puddle. Someone carried me back inside the mess, removed my wet jacket, collar and tie and then took me to the first aid post outside the mess; where Len was lying 'spark out on the floor'. They laid me beside him and poured buckets of water over us. Apparently I got up with arms waving doing swimming strokes and just disappeared into the gloom of the night. Obviously, with radar still intact, I was on my way to the billet when I had passed out in the field.

29/30th December, 1943; BERLIN

The Christmas celebrations had been but a mere bright interlude in Bomber Command's ever darkening war of attrition, for on the night of Wednesday 29th December, Berlin's flak torn skies once again beckoned.

Over 700 bombers approached Berlin from the south and it was the south eastern part of the city that received the heaviest bombing. The 15 Lancasters from Fiskerton found the city once again covered in cloud.

I had reported sick on Boxing Day as I could hardly walk and was admitted to the sick quarters with water on the knee (or was it whisky?). I was told I would be in for about a week. On the 29th December my crew were on this operation - they had to take a 'spare Wop/Ag', called Thomson, in my place.

That evening I was in tormented anguish– I heard the Lancs go out around 17.00hrs and during their absence I could not sleep a wink. They returned about midnight but even then I had a restless night.

The following morning one of the visitors to the sick quarters said that a crew was missing from the previous night, when I asked who it was, he said he thought it was 'Young's crew' - I was absolutely stunned with disbelief. For the rest of the day I remained in a state of semi shock until later my boisterous crew paid me a visit without a care in the world - I don't remember if I laughed or cried...perhaps both. The duff gen given by the visitor proved to be totally incorrect as no 49 Squadron aircraft were missing.

However, Bomber Command did lose 20 aircraft on the raid.

Johnny and the boys gave the following de-brief; *"Take-off 16.57hrs. Berlin 20.22hrs at 20,000ft in 5th wave. 10/10ths cloud. Centre of 4 red/green stars in sights. Run up on 1 cluster of 4 flares. PFF very good and on time. Raid seemed well concentrated. Landed 00.17hrs."*

On New Years day I was discharged from hospital and found I was on ops that night. Target - Berlin again.

1/2nd January, 1944 ; BERLIN

New year 1944 was heralded in with Bomber Command's ninth attack in the series on Berlin. An all Lancaster force found the target was, as usual, covered by cloud which disrupted any possible concentration of fires. Fiskerton had dispatched 15 bombers but P/O Jock Simpson and crew (JB466) were forced to return early due to petrol leaking from their port inner engine.

The Dickinson crew in E-Easy (ND383) on their very first

op were attacked by two Me 109s; after only short bursts both the mid-upper and rear turret's guns froze up in the Lancaster. With only verbal instructions from his gunners the pilot managed to evade the fighters and a successful sortie was completed.

Sgt Meggison and crew (JB710) sustained flak damage whilst fending off the attentions of yet another night fighter - they too managed to complete their sortie and returned safely to Fiskerton's FIDO runway.

We were once again in the last wave and would be one of the last to drop our bombs. Approximately half way to the target the radar navigation equipment (H2S) failed. We had no astro navigation or ground visibility due to cloud cover above and below. The wind speed and direction sent back by the Pathfinders, and re-broadcast to the main force by Group HQ, may have altered as we became completely lost. Eventually, the cloud below us thinned out and we were able to pin-point our position as being many miles away from Berlin and we were already past our time for bombing.

Replying to the pilot's question, "Should we go on to the target (being this late we would be on our own) or turn back and pick a secondary target?", we all agreed that we should go and look at the situation. On arriving over Berlin some 20 minutes late there were huge fires but no flak, no searchlights or fighter flares (possibly they had all stood down believing the raid was over). There were still some marker flares so the bomb aimer selected his target, and dropped our bombs.

We headed for home as fast as we could, hoping to catch up with the tail enders. Approaching Hanover we were bracketed by predicted flak, being the only aircraft in that part of the sky meant that they were shooting at US and it was both fascinating as well as frightening - four bursts of shells in a line followed by another four even closer. The skipper had to outguess the gunners and try to put the aircraft in a spot where there would be no shell bursts. We were lucky, he managed to dodge every set of bursts and the only damage was about an inch lost off the tip of the port inner propeller blade.

Of the 421 Lancasters sent to Berlin, 28 failed to return with the majority falling to the high flying Me 110s. All 49's aircraft returned to base. Due to snow falling heavily and poor visibility conditions it was decided to ignite FIDO. As crews tumbled out onto their dispersals the first light of Sunday morning was struggling to get through the dawn gloom.

We were greeted by our faithful ground crew and none of us thought that ops would be 'on the cards again tonight' as the snow quickly began to settle. How wrong could we be!

In the stillness of a white-carpeted winter's morning our devoted WAAF driver nervously negotiated her way around a quickly disappearing peri-track.

We were blissfully unaware that this was the very last time that we would make this return journey...for as we settled down for a well earned kip, every available bod on camp was commandeered into clearing the runway in preparation for the night's operation....Berlin again no doubt!

2/3rd January, 1944; BERLIN

Despite the worsening weather, it was decided to mount yet another operation to Berlin. Thanks to the strenuous efforts of the station personnel Fiskerton was able to launch 12 Lancasters from the 13 detailed with take-off beginning at 15 minutes before midnight.

With such a short turn around time between this and the previous night's operation, Bomber Command could only put up 383 aircraft. Of these, icing conditions forced many of the main force crews to jettison parts of their loads in order to gain precious height. Just 311 bombers struggled to reach a cloud covered Berlin where the bombing was spread with no concentrated fires developing.

The German controllers soon realised the target in advance and instructed the night-fighters accordingly; many of the 27 Lancasters lost fell in the Berlin area.

Flying in our regular aircraft JB231 'Nancy Pants' (or officially 'Bandlaw N-Nan') we took off at four minutes to midnight on a freezing cold night. As we had landed in the early hours of that morning, we were on our way back to Berlin for the second time within 24 hours. Stretching a point, but nevertheless, correctly stated. Just before take-off the ground crew boys stowed their forage caps just inside the entrance door... one of their little rituals.

We set course and approximately two and a half hours later reached the final turning point about 60 miles north west of Berlin. 'Fishpond' (downward facing radar detection unit) was for once working well and I was monitoring for enemy aircraft below us. The screen showed literally hundreds of blips most of which were heading in the same direction. However, there was no way of identifying which were friendly.

When we reached the turning point, the Skipper dipped the starboard wing to make the turn... suddenly without warning there was a terrific crash. I was thrown violently sideways out of my seat losing my helmet and oxygen mask as I fell to the floor. Quickly scrambling up I looked out of the astrodome just in time to see a large part of the starboard wing peel away together with the outboard engine. As they disappeared into the darkness behind I glimpsed what appeared to be another Lancaster passing below at the rear.

This was later confirmed by Spud, the mid upper gunner, who had witnessed the impact from his turret. It would appear that this other Lancaster had already turned onto the new course to the target and was cutting back across the bomber stream when it struck our starboard wing.

We believe that its cockpit struck between our two starboard engines.

Remember the song that Doreen was singing when we met her during our leave - 'Coming In On A Wing and A Prayer', was that an omen?

Painting by John Ward depicting the damage to Nancy Pants.

Here we were over Northern Germany with two thirds of our starboard wing and an engine missing, the inboard engine damaged and falling to pieces.

That song was surely meant for us!

Flying at around 20,000 feet at the time of the collision and having lost my helmet and oxygen mask I was unable to communicate with the skipper or crew. Also, with no oxygen I would pass out after only a short time.

It would seem that the extra training that we did in the static fuselage at Swinderby came into effect... or was it self preservation? Whatever it was, my 'auto pilot' must have kicked in. I grabbed my parachute and was climbing over the main spar when the skipper started to pull the aircraft out of its steep dive and I became stuck to the spar by the G force. It seemed like many minutes before I was able to move but was probably only a few seconds.

As I made my way down the dark fuselage I noted that Spud's turret was empty and as I reached the exit saw that it was open with the door secured back and both gunners standing there with their parachutes clipped on ready to jump. Without having received a specific instruction to abandon the aircraft, but following our training, as number one to go and maybe given a sign by one of the gunners, I sat crouched on the step facing forward and rolled out.

I have no recollection of clipping the parachute onto my harness or counting to ten or even pulling the rip cord, all I remember was hanging beneath the canopy watching the aircraft in what appeared to be normal flight, disappearing into the darkness. I saw no other parachutes and seriously wondered if they were going to make it back home leaving me behind. Was it a Court Martial offence to abandon an aircraft without permission or just a charge of Absent Without Leave?

In truth, I was in a state of shock, I had left the aircraft and was now on my own hanging from a parachute descending into enemy territory with no idea what the fate of my crew was or what lay ahead.

FTR JB231	F/O	J.E.M.	Young RCAF	Pilot	(P.o.W.)
(EA-N)	Sgt	A.W.	Vidow	F/E	(P.o.W.)
'B Flt'	F/O	J.	Scott RCAF	NAV	(P.o.W.)
	Sgt	E.B.	Cachart	W/OP	(P.o.W.)
	Sgt	M.	Mahony RAAF	A/G	(P.o.W.)
Crew on their	P/O	L.M.	Orchard	B/A	(P.o.W.)
8th operation	Sgt	L.	Crossman	A/G	(P.o.W.)

Note: Len Crossman was unfortunately killed in a motor cycle accident in 1945, an ironic twist of fate after surviving the war. Jack Scott died in 1996.

FTR JB727	F/L	C.J.E.	Palmer	Pilot	(Killed)
(EA-S)	Sgt	P.O.	Camm	F/E	(Killed)
'B Flt'	F/O	G.T.	Young	NAV	(Killed)
	Sgt	H.	Conrad	W/OP	(Killed)
	Sgt	D.D.R.	Dallaway	A/G	(Killed)
Crew on their	F/O	R.	Stobo	A/B	(Killed)
11th operation	Sgt	D.F.	Prusher	A/G	(Killed)

Note:

JB231 was on its 13th operation as N-Nan ‘Nancy Pants’ having been transferred from ‘A’ flight where it did 6 operations as ‘B’ Baker.

John Ward painted two pictures of the this aircraft, ’One Wing And A Prayer’ and ‘Nancy Pants Last Flight’ as can be seen on pages 98 and 160.

14

UNINVITED GUESTS

The Wop/Ag's position in the Lancaster was the warmest, with heat from the engines piped into this area. With the door behind the main spar closed it warmed the whole cockpit ranging from very warm in my position to very

For you, the war is over !!
Cartoon from the book, Handle With Care by Ex Prisoners of War, Andy Anderson and Dave Westmacott

cool in the nose. Consequently, I flew in just my battle dress and sweater plus flying boots (the metal floor was very cold). The other members of the crew would wear varying layers of clothing depending upon their position in the aircraft, the bomb aimer being the coldest of the five in the forward area. The two gunners would have long underwear, sweater, battledress, electrically heated inner suit, a thick outer suit, silk gloves under leather gauntlets and probably two pairs of thick socks in their fur lined flying boots. I never gave a thought to what I would do in an emergency - I was about to find out.

It was extremely cold... rain mixed with snow driven by the 80 mph winds that had been forecast at briefing was stinging my exposed face and hands as well as making the parachute oscillate badly. As it spilled air I dropped suddenly until the canopy refilled and again was able to slow my descent. I tried to control the oscillations by pulling down on the harness straps but my bare wet hands began to freeze to the straps and I had to let go. I stuffed them into my pockets to warm them up only to have to control the oscillations all over again. My left leg, weakened by my fall on Christmas Eve, became severely cramped and I could do nothing to ease the excruciating pain.

The descent seemed to last forever but eventually I saw some darker patches below me. I was thinking that I was about to come out below the cloud when my boots suddenly crashed through the branches of a large tree. My descent was abruptly halted and there I hung, suspended by my parachute harness, somewhere in a dark forest in Germany.

It was so dark that I had no way of gauging how far I was from the ground. Unwilling to just press the release box and take my chances it took numerous attempts before I eventually managed to swing myself close enough to grasp the tree trunk with my good leg. Releasing my harness and with arms and leg wrapped round the trunk I carefully slid down all of about four feet and was sitting on the ground.

By now I was soaked to the skin, shivering uncontrollably with cold... lost, bewildered and in shock but still on 'auto'.

I realised I had to find shelter soon. Hobbling, crawling and sliding down a steep slope through the pitch dark forest I eventually came to a clearing and then a few yards more to a wire fence with what looked like a small river on the other side. Certainly it looked a different shade and there were no trees visible along its length. Kneeling down I reached through and found it was a sand track which I presumed was a forest fire break. I hobbled along using the fence for support and finally came to a road. I have no idea how far I had travelled to this point or to the farmhouse that I later came to.

With the freezing conditions, snow and sleet, soaking wet and hardly able to walk, any thought of evading capture was out of the question.

I went up to the farmhouse, sat on the doorstep and banged with my fist on the door. After some time I saw a small flickering light through a crack in the door and a male voice shouting something which I believe told me to go away. Then the light disappeared. As I was in no condition to go any further and in urgent need of shelter I banged again and again until the door was opened by a middle aged woman holding a candle. I was hunched on the doorstep and holding my sheath knife by the tip of the blade, offering it to her in an act of submission. She took it and helped me up and supported me as she lead me into a ground floor bedroom.

Her husband was in bed and laid there glaring at me as his wife pulled out a chair for me to sit on. As I was still shivering and my teeth chattering she fetched a blanket and put it round my shoulders. She then removed a sliver of wood that had penetrated through the palm of my hand, bathed and then dressed the wound with some of the bandage from my knee that I had removed as the wetness made it much too tight. She gave me a towel to dry my face and hair and then gave me a drink of cold coffee.

I had some Craven A tipped cigarettes in my metal cigarette case and although these were slightly damp from my wet battle dress I offered one to the husband. He got out of bed, took one out of the case and locked it in a glass cabinet. (I often wondered if he was saving it for victory day).

Gradually warmth began to penetrate and blood flowed into my fingers and toes making then tingle. Meanwhile, a daughter had been sent to the local Burgermeister. As we waited, although we could not communicate verbally they were able to convey to me, by showing me a photograph of a young man dressed in naval uniform with a black naval cap ribbon draped over the frame, together with various gesticulations, that they had lost a son who served on a U-boat. Later, when I was able to think more clearly and reflect on the unexpected care and consideration she had shown, I realised that as a mother she was treating me the way she hoped her own son would have been treated in similar circumstances.

It must have been around 3.15am when a car arrived to collect me. I was helped into the back seat and driven a few miles to the Burgermeister's house. He stood in the lounge with a shotgun under his arm as his wife lead me into the dining area where we all sat down at the table. The shot gun was placed on the surface, but well out of my reach. The wife spoke very good English and began questioning me as to how we were shot down, what height were we flying etc.

She also wanted to know if it was by flak or night fighter and where were my crew etc. I told her (tongue in cheek) 27,000 feet, but nothing more. Within half an hour a Luftwaffe Corporal and Private arrived to collect me and as I left the lady handed me an apple. The car they were in had just two seats with a Dicky seat outside at the back. As I was already soaked I offered to sit there but with a big smile the Corporal wagged his finger and said, "Nein, nein." So I sat in the warmth of the passenger seat with the private sitting outside in the cold and rain.

I was driven to a local Luftwaffe station and handed over to the Feldwebel (NCO). He was alone and we both sat in the warmth of the guardroom. Again, the language barrier meant we could not converse but we seemed to get on quite well together, certainly he showed me no animosity. Around 6.00 am he got out his rations, cut everything in half and shared them with me, then made some coffee that we drank black and unsweetened, but still welcome. At about 8.00 am after putting me in a cell, he shook my hand saying what I took to be, "Good Luck", locked the door and went off duty.

Later that morning five Luftwaffe Officers came into my cell and I had a moment or two of consternation, wondering what was going to happen next. One of them walked up to me, reached forward and with a smile he patted me on the shoulder, holding up his other hand with fingers spread apart and said, "Liverpool funf (five) times." Then another did the same, "London acht (eight) times" and another, who spoke some English said, "You are lucky, your war is over... we have to fight on." I was still in a state of shock and here I was, in company with the enemy. As they were all laughing and very friendly it took some time before I realised that we were all just aircrew but in different uniforms. As with the Feldwebel, no animosity or the bitter hatred I had expected.

Many years later I felt that it was likely that these first few Germans that I met were typical of a very large number of the population who, like us, did not want war but were led or even forced to follow the dictates of our respective government's propaganda campaigns. The fact that there was no ill treatment from these initial contacts enabled me to ignore some of the hostility that I later encountered as a PoW.

Later that day, with two guards, I was taken by car to another Luftwaffe station. This was somewhere north of Neubrandenburg that I now know was Trollenhagen (see later in the story). Here I was interviewed by the Commanding Officer. He showed me my 10 inch sheath knife and wanted to know why I carried it in my flying boot. I told him that it was from my boy scout days and that I used it to open the tins of fresh orange juice that we carried on operations. (Quite true.)

He accepted this (but did not give me the knife back!) and after more questioning I was taken away to a nearby low building which contained a row of cells. I was placed in one of them and left alone to ponder what was going to happen next... I was still wearing the **red silk scarf**.

My thoughts were obviously very mixed, trying to come to terms with such a sudden change in circumstances… what had happened to my crew.. had they got back home.. had they crashed and had any survived... how long would I be a prisoner.. how would I be treated? Although I cannot claim to remember it I am sure that I also wondered when I would get something to eat.

It was very cold so I took advantage of the clever design of the 'escape type' flying boots. These had suede leggings stitched to the 'shoes' and lined with thick lambs wool. A small pen knife, concealed in the lining, enabled you to cut the stitching and remove the legging portion to leave you with normal looking shoes. I cut the leggings off and put them inside my shirt at the back and front with the soft lambs wool against my skin.

It has only just occurred to me that the knife in the leggings 'pocket', which the Germans must have known existed, had been missed in the searches up to this point.

The next day, Spud and Len, the two gunners, and Les, the bomb aimer, were brought in and put in adjacent cells.

This gave me both pleasure that they had survived (and that I had not jumped too soon) and sadness that they too were going to be PoWs. Spud had been carried in on a stretcher having hurt his back. Orch told me that he landed on grass (I believe the only one not to land in a tree). He wandered around in the darkness, eventually found a road and saw a light moving along it. It was a man wheeling his bicycle. Les followed and next thing was a hand on his shoulder and he was marched through a gate and into a guard room. Next morning he was taken by car to a large house in another village. On entering, the lady of the house said, "Good Morning", in quite normal English. He was ushered into a room where he saw Len sitting by the fire. Len told him that he had also wandered around in the dark, found this long high wall but could not find a door or gate. He settled in some shelter and went to sleep but was woken by a dog barking after which a man took him into the house.

Both Orch and Len were then taken through the village to what Orch thought was a police station (possibly a small lock up) and there laying on the floor was Spud. Orch thought that he was dead but fortunately he wasn't. After some delay they lifted Spud, on the stretcher, into the back of a lorry. With two guards with Len and Orch they were driven to Trollenhagen where they joined me in the cell block.

Like me, Spud had landed in a tree but had released his harness and dropped some distance onto a pile of logs that were stacked at the tree's base, seriously hurting his back. He managed to get to a road and sat there until daylight in his flying suit with his face stained with brown anti-frost cream.

He was quite short in stature and yet wide in his padded suit and with his brown streaked face he must have looked a strange sight. Sometime after dawn a German cycled up the road and as he passed by Spud waved and called out, "Hoy." The German replied with, "Hoy", waved and cycled on. He presumably reported his sighting of a 'brown gnome' or a 'terrorflieger' as police turned up shortly afterwards and captured Spud. (It was not until Spud returned to Australia that it was found that he had cracked his spine and he has had to wear a special support harness all his life.)

The following day the navigator, Scotty and flight engineer, Alan arrived. They had both individually walked some miles away from the crash area but were captured later that day. On the third day the skipper, Johnny, who had been taken to a hospital with a dislocated shoulder was brought in and the whole crew were together again. We had no way of knowing what had happened to the crew of the other Lancaster. Alan recently reminded me that Spud had told him that after I jumped, Len was sitting on the step and hesitating so Spud pushed him out with his boot and dived out after him.

This was Spud's second escape from a Lancaster crash in five weeks.

15

DULAG LUFT

With three guards we travelled by train in a luxury second class compartment, with toilet en-suite, to Hamburg. We had been issued with some food for the journey and one item, like a fish cake but translucent with a yellow core, smelled of a combination of fish and bad eggs. It was so strong that I threw mine away at some point thinking it inedible, little did I know that I would come to look forward to future issues later.

We disembarked at Hamburg and were taken to a civilian jail for the night. The cell, which was below ground, was very damp and cold with nothing but a square hole in the corner for a toilet. We huddled together for warmth and had a sleepless night. Next morning, with the same three guards, we were driven to the railway station. Whilst waiting on the platform for the train the guards positioned us in the angle of two buildings and stood with their backs to us to protect us from the angry Germans who stood and shouted abuse until our train arrived. As the train trundled its way along many miles of track out of Hamburg we became aware of the very large number of burnt out and badly damaged buildings resulting from the heavy bombing raids. It was no wonder the guards needed to protect us from the crowds at the railway station.

This train took us to Frankfurt En Maine where we caught a tram to Oberusal and Dulag Luft, the interrogation centre. We all had to strip whilst our clothes and naked bodies were searched for escape material (Yes, they DID search the naked body - an escape compass was small enough to hide). They confiscated all other banned items as well as some personal bits like pens, watches etc. In my speedy exit from the aircraft my 'escape kit' (a small pack containing German and French bank notes, silk map of Europe, water purification, compressed chocolate and Horlicks tablets) was left in the cockpit. Surprisingly, I was allowed to keep the leggings of my flying boots and the **red silk scarf**.

We were put into individual cells. These had frosted glass windows, a single iron bed with a straw mattress and two thin blankets. They were fitted with electric heaters that could only be controlled from outside in the corridor. There was also a device with an arm similar to a small railway signal that dropped down when the control catch was released. It protruded into the corridor to indicate that you needed to visit the toilet or needed a guard for something. Then, with luck, after not too long a delay a guard would come and see what you wanted or escort you to the toilet and then back to the cell.

From time to time the guards would turn the heat up high making the cell overbearingly hot so you stripped off to keep cool or they would turn it off so you donned every item of clothing and climbed under the two blankets to keep warm. Possibly this was a deliberate attempt to make our stay so uncomfortable that we would answer all their questions in the (false) belief that doing so would get us released more quickly... which in fact was just the opposite... the more you said the longer you stayed. Every prisoner received a visit from a man dressed in black and with a `Red Cross' armband. He would politely ask you to complete a form that would be sent to Geneva who would then notify the English authorities that you were safe and now a PoW. This form started off quite innocently, asking for name, rank, number and next of kin, but then went on to ask for details of squadron, aircraft type etc.

You were supposed to sign at the bottom but having been pre-warned of the interrogation tactics I don't think many did,

I didn't. The German became very angry, shouting and stamping his jackboots and abusing me for being so stupid.

The actual interrogation took place daily, with the usual questions about squadron, aircraft, bomb loads etc. to which you answered with nothing except name, rank and number.

Sessions lasted approximately 30 to 60 minutes, the rest of the day being spent alone in the cell. Food was of miniscule quantity consisting of (if I remember correctly) ersatz coffee and a slice of black bread in the morning, a bowl of thin soup mid-day and another slice of bread and coffee in the evening. Certainly not enough for healthy young men.

After four days I was let out and transferred to the nearby transit camp where I met up with two or three members of the crew, the others joined us the following day. We had to wait until there were sufficient numbers to make up a shipment before being transported to a PoW camp. We were introduced to our first meal of Red Cross food. How wonderful it tasted after the black bread and thin soup of the last few days.

The German rations were totally insufficient to overcome the constant pangs of hunger that we suffered, we did not realise that this would be part of our daily lives from now on.

There were three main types of parcel, British, Canadian and American. The British parcel contents varied which gave the prisoner the pleasure of anticipation when opening one. Although the food content of the Canadian and American differed considerably in style, they were generally the same other than the cigarettes which would be either 100 cheap unknown or 60 of a well known brand. Getting a different type of parcel every few weeks gave us a varied diet.

As I received very few American parcels I have only a vague idea of their contents. I think that these were based on the standard 'K' rations issued to troops in the field.

Some of the contents that might be found in a British Red Cross parcel;

1/4lb packet of tea

Cocoa powder

Bar of chocolate

Tinned pudding

Tin of meat roll (Lacked flavour, add jam and eat as sweet)

Tin of compressed oats (Very good, made many servings)

Tin of processed cheese

Tin of condensed milk

Tin of dried eggs

Tin of sardines or herrings

Tin of preserve

Tin of margarine

Tin of sugar

Tin of vegetables

Tin of biscuits

Packet of dried fruit

(prunes or sultanas)

Bar of soap

A typical; English Red Cross food parcel

The contents of the Canadian parcels included a large tin of butter, some very hard biscuits, a tin of salmon and a tin of excellent powdered milk called KLIM (spell it backwards). This tin is mentioned later as it was a very versatile container which, with a little imagination and a lot of ingenuity, became one of the most useful items in any PoW camp.

16

STALAG 4B 'MULHBERG'

The three officers in the crew, skipper Johnny, navigator Scotty and bomb aimer Les said goodbye to us after about a week and with some other officers they were shipped off to Stalag Luft 3, the Officers Camp, at Sagan. We four NCOs with possibly 150 others went by cattle trucks to Stalag 4B at Mulhberg.

This was our first experience of travel in this way, there were numerous cattle trucks which had the words 8 Chevaux 40 Hommes printed on the side. So horses, although bigger, had considerably more room than humans !

There were close to 40 prisoners plus a few guards to each truck. The whole centre section, opposite the sliding doors, was reserved for the guards, separated from the prisoners by a wire 'wall' with a flimsy door into the fore and aft sections.

The guards area took up a quarter of the whole truck with around twenty men crammed into each of the remaining sections. There was not enough room for everyone to lie down so we took it in turns with some sitting hunched up whilst others lay, packed close together like sardines. There was a small window high up on one side, too small for anyone to climb through but still protected by the dreaded 'barbed wire' that would keep us fenced in for the foreseeable future. Our introduction to prison camp life awaited us when we finally disembarked from the train. A Wehrmacht Oberfeldwebel in a long green overcoat and 'jackboots' stamped along examining each one of us. I noticed that he looked at each man's footwear, most of them wore the escape type flying boots with trousers tucked into the tops.

When he got to me he saw only the shoes. He lifted my trouser leg up, revealing that they were the lower part of my escape boots......he ripped open my battle dress jacket and pulled out the leggings and then back-handed me very hard around my face as he swore at me for damaging the boots. We were lead into a hut where everyone had to remove their boots which were replaced with wooden clogs. It was believed that the flying boots were sent to the Russian front or maybe became guards 'booty'. The clogs had no heels so easily slipped off your feet and due to the boggy conditions of the grassless mud you frequently had to walk bare footed and carry the clogs... but I still retained my **red silk scarf.**

Stalag 4B was run by the Wehrmacht as it contained mainly Allied Army personnel captured in the Middle East, there being approximately 6000 Army to 1000 RAF PoWs. The RAF PoWs had a separate compound but when we arrived this was full so we were put in with the Army lads where we were outnumbered by about 10 to 1. There were some 200 PoWs in each hut, sleeping in three tier bunks that covered about four-fifths of the area down one side, the open area contained tables, benches and three rectangular stoves. These stoves were about 6 feet long by 30 inches wide with a chimney at one end and the fire door at the other. They provided both heat and cooking as the flat top could be used as a hob. The hottest part was close to the chimney so as soon as one person's food was cooked and removed, others' pots and pans were quickly shuffled toward the chimney.

It was about 6 or 8 weeks later, at the evening roll call, that my name was called out and I was told to pack my things and be ready to leave in the morning. No reason was given and the only conclusion arrived at by some more experienced prisoners was that I had been commissioned and was going to the officers' camp. Nobody suggested I was going to be shot.

17

DULAG LUFT... AGAIN!

Next morning I was taken by a guard to the main gate where I was handed over to an English speaking Luftwaffe Corporal and a Private. The corporal said that I was being returned to Dulag Luft for further interrogation. He was very pleasant but warned that if I tried to escape he would not hesitate to shoot me, however, there was no reason why we should not enjoy the rather long journey. In fact he was very knowledgeable and pointed out many landmarks and places of interest as we travelled by a circuitous route back to Frankfurt En Maine. The last leg of the journey was at night with a two hour wait for a change of trains at one station.

Our connection was apparently delayed so I was taken into a Services Canteen which was full of German servicemen. They all stopped talking and stared as the Corporal led me between the packed tables and into a rear room, then he sent the Private to fetch food and drink for the three of us.

When our train arrived, I was once again taken through the crowded canteen which again fell silent as we passed through. Boarding the train, the Corporal and I passed down the corridor and into a compartment where I sat between him and another passenger.

After we had been travelling a short time, this passenger lit a cigarette and I sensed that in the light from the match he was looking at me... then in a broad north eastern 'Geordie' type accent he asked me where I was from. It transpired that he was in the Royal Army Medical Corps and wore a Red Cross arm band that hopefully gave him some protection. He was escorting a Serbian Officer, who had been tortured by the Gestapo, back to camp. He had been shot through the palms of each hand and now had the mentality of a child.

He offered me some cigarettes but as I had my Red Cross parcel and cigarettes I declined, assuming they would only be taken from me when we got to Dulag. I never saw one, but I presumed he had a guard with him. What were the chances of sitting next to another Englishman in a railway carriage in the middle of the night in central Germany during the war? I have often wondered if he survived.

At Dulag Luft I was once again strip searched before being put into a cell but to my surprise, as I was now a registered PoW, I was allowed to keep my Red Cross food parcel and other bits that I had accumulated in the few weeks at Stalag 4B. A strange situation, in solitary confinement yet able to retain toiletries, Red Cross food and cigarettes, and the **red silk scarf**.

For four days I was interrogated by a very aggressive officer who made me stand the whole time. Each session lasted between one and two hours with questions about a radio they had found in the wreckage of our Lancaster. On the fifth day there was no interrogation but on the sixth, with a different officer, interrogation resumed. He told me that the previous officer had gone on compassionate leave as some of his family had been killed in an air raid. Was this true or was it part of the interrogation technique in the hope that I would give the answers to their questions? Whatever, this session was certainly different, being the gentle approach... I was allowed to sit, smoke (his cigarettes) and it was very friendly but questioning continued about the radio equipment. The Germans were referring to some new equipment used for jamming radar which had been fitted in N-Nan whilst I was in hospital. I had been given some very brief instructions which went something like this. There was a switch and red light fitted to my work desk. I was to switch it on when we crossed English coast and the red light would glow. If it changed to flashing I turned the unit off, waited 15 minutes and then switched on again. I knew nothing about the equipment or where in the fuselage it had been installed.

On the tenth day the interrogation Officer told me that I would be going to the transit camp the next day and that I would not be going back to Stalag 4B but to a much better camp, Luft 6 at Heydekrug in Lithuania. He asked no further questions but was happy to sit and talk for some time.

I asked him if it was possible to obtain any information about my friend, Tom Brady, who had been posted missing in November. I gave him his name, rank and number and he looked up some records and told me that he and the crew had been killed and where they were buried. (The first of the Musketeers to die.) I got the impression that he did not like doing this job... he wished me good luck and next day I was sent to the transit camp.

In later years I obtained the following information from the RAF Historical Branch:-

"Sgt T G Brady was the wireless operator/air gunner in Lancaster Bomber DV388 on No. 626 Sqdn RAF and based at RAF Wickenby. DV388 was part of a force of 450 aircraft consisting of 443 Lancasters and 7 Mosquitoes despatched on a raid to Berlin on the night of 26th November 1943.

The raid destroyed 38 war industry factories and damaged many more. 28 Lancasters failed to return from this raid and 14 more crashed on landing.

Unfortunately the circumstances of how this aircraft met its fate are unknown. Presumably the aircraft crashed due to enemy action over the target area.

The full crew are as follows:-

R109235	*F/Sgt*	*C J E*	*Kindt*	*Pilot*	*RCAF*
R148889	*F/Sgt*	*R R*	*Small*	*Navigator*	*RCAF*
1319845	*Sgt*	*T G*	*Brady*	*WOP/AG*	*RAF*
1480159	*Sgt*	*E*	*Calloway*	*F/Engineer*	*RAF*
R153012	*Sgt*	*A S*	*Macdonald*	*Bomb Aimer*	*RCAF*
1116830	*Sgt*	*C*	*Johnson*	*Upper Gunner*	*RAF*
1851986	*Sgt*	*F*	*Matthews*	*Rear Gunner*	*RAF*

All are buried in the Berlin War Cemetery. Plot A, Row J, grave 22"

Athos, the first of the Musketeers to fall in battle.

After a few days in the transit camp, with many new PoWs, we were loaded into cattle trucks once again and began something like a ten day journey. After a few days travelling we stopped in sidings whilst an air raid was in progress. Like the previous journey to Stalag 4B the conditions in the trucks was just as uncomfortable, made even worse as the journey was so much longer. Having been a prisoner for a couple of months I was continually being questioned about conditions in a camp, what was the food like, etc. I could only tell them about the camp at 4B but had been able to describe the contents of the Red Cross food parcels that, supplies permitting, we got each week… there was nothing left of the one I had in the cells... and none were issued for the journey.

18

LUFT VI 'HEYDEKRUG'

Some ten days later we arrived at Stalag Luft 6 at Heydekrug near Memel on the Lithuania border and I was more surprised than the others at the difference between this one and 4B. It was an all RAF PoW camp with three lagars (compounds) with approximately 2500 men in each of A and K Lagars and about 1000 in the third 'American' lagar.

I was in 'A' Lagar where there were four long huts divided into nine rooms. (see cartoon sketch.) The huts were A B C & D and there was just one spare bed in room D7 into which I moved. Many of the prisoners were 'old sweats' from the early days of the war and as is not unusual in these circumstances I was made welcome. Unfortunately the bunk was minus bed boards (slats). A shout went up for the thick string that secured the British Red Cross parcels. Odd lengths appeared and Jock McGregor and another PoW quickly 'knitted' a net hammock from these bits (rather like making a fishing net). This they secured to the top of the four corner posts of the bunk and I had a hammock... possibly the most comfortable bed in the hut.

I have to record that one prisoner in the hut, Philip Blackburn, a Fairey Battle pilot who had been shot down early in the war, was the first to ask me if I needed anything and quickly presented me with tooth brush, comb and a razor. A very generous gesture bearing in mind that any surplus items could have been sold for many cigarettes. Thank you Philip!

I think it was about the middle of March 1944 that a new batch of prisoners arrived. One was F/Sgt Fred 'Hugo' Hughes, the bomb aimer in 'Musketeer' Bill Dykes crew, and he gave me the news that Bill was believed to have gone down with the aircraft. Again, as in the case of Tom, post war I received the following from the RAF Air Historical Branch:-

"Sergeant William Arthur Dykes was the Wireless Operator / Air Gunner in Lancaster Bomber No. DV220 on 166 Sqdn RAF and based at RAF Kirmington. The aircraft was part of a force of 823 aircraft - 561 Lancasters, 255 Halifaxes and 7 Mosquitoes tasked to bomb Leipzig on the night of 19th February 1944. Due to heavy cloud over the target and the American bombing of the area on the following day the outcome of that particular raid is unknown, however 44 Lancasters and 24 Halifaxes were lost. Whilst approaching the target, DV220 was attacked by night fighters, four crew members successfully baled out.

The full crew are as follows:-

R141695	*F/Sgt*	*F F G*	*Allan*	*Pilot*	*RCAF*
J85960	*P/O*	*J J*	*Yelland*	*Navigator*	*RCAF*
1575431	*Sgt*	*W A*	*Dykes*	*Wireless/Ag*	*RAF*
1157645	*Sgt*	*T H*	*Lee*	*Flight Engineer*	*RAF*
R165160	*F/Sgt*	*F I*	*Hughes*	*Bomb Aimer*	*RCAF*
1087197	*F/Sgt*	*J N*	*Manuel*	*Upper Gunner*	*RAF*
1818912	*Sgt*	*A*	*Rose*	*Rear Gunner*	*RAF*

F/Sgt F F G Allan is buried in the Berlin War Cemetery, Plot 8, Row K, Grave 12. P/O J J Yelland is remembered on the Runnymede Memorial (Panel 253) as is Sgt W A Dykes (Panel 228). The rest of the crew were all captured by the Germans and returned safely to the UK in May 1945."

Aramis, the second of the Musketeers to fall in battle.

Stalag Luft 6 was very different from Stalag 4B... it was so well organised. Each room had a man appointed in charge and he was the person whom you informed if you had any plans or ideas about how to escape, or any other problems. There was an 'escape committee' but I never knew who they were. In each camp a `Man of Confidence' would be appointed, selected from and by the prisoners and approved by the Germans. We were extremely fortunate to have Warrant Officer (Dixie) Deans as ours.

I am sure that all the prisoners in this camp will agree with me that he never received adequate recognition for the excellent work that he did, and the extra benefits that he obtained from the Germans on our behalf.

1944 was a wonderful hot summer... the constant supply of Red Cross food parcels, an essential supplement to the German food ration in maintaining a reasonable standard of fitness, continued uninterrupted.

Without these, as we would learn later, the meagre amounts issued by the Germans would have brought us down to almost starvation level. However, things were as good as we could expect and sporting activities were one of the main outdoor pursuits. I was never very keen on playing football but did get to learn and play a little rugby.

As the area for sports, which doubled as a parade ground, was limited for space only one game of cricket, football, or rugby etc could be played at any one time. Obviously there were many spectators. One activity that was very popular, introduced by the Canadians who played softball, was playing 'catch'. Any two or more would wear a 'catcher's mitt' and throw the fairly hard ball, often as hard as they could, for the others to catch. Later we also played baseball, which was introduced by the Americans.

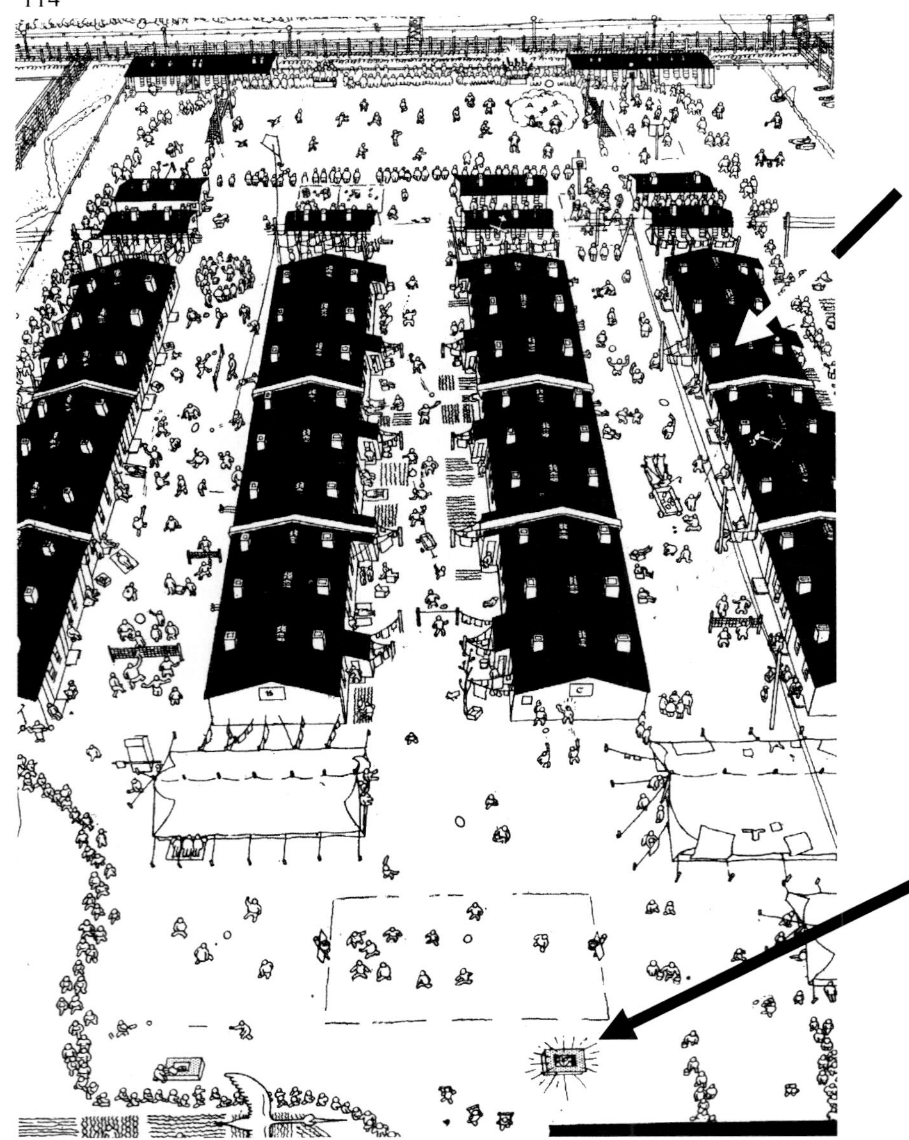

'A' Lager Heydekrug Luft VI with approximately 2500 prisoners in this small area. Arrows point to items mentioned in text.

The picture on the opposite page is taken from the book 'Handle With Care' that contains sketches drawn by artists Andy Anderson and Dave Westmacott, and carried by them from camp to camp. You have to look carefully to see all the activities that they have tried to include. At the bottom right you will see a part of a single hut... this was the communal cookhouse in front of which is a small rectangle (arrowed) - a brick incinerator with a hole in the concrete top for the smoke to escape. This was cleaned out and used by Larry Slattery to practice his violin. Larry was taken prisoner, together with another crew member Georgie Booth, on the second day of the war, and they were the PoWs who served the longest time being released in April 1945. The upper arrow shows where I lived in D7.

One point that you may not appreciate is that in the confined area of a PoW camp, there is NOWHERE where you can be alone or have moments of absolute silence. Even in the middle of the night, with 60 men in a hut sleeping in two tier bunks there are coughs and sneezes, groans, moans and even the occasional nightmare. One learned to live and cope with the small irritations from others as they coped with yours.

Sadly a further meeting of new prisoners brought bad news. Sgt A (Alan) Ferguson, mid upper gunner and T/Sgt W E (Bill) Steeper, (USAAF) bomb aimer from the crew of the third Musketeer, Jimmy Goddard arrived. The post-war information that was received from the RAF Air Historical Branch said:-

"Our records show that Sgt Alan Arthur Frank Goddard was the Wireless Operator / Air Gunner in Lancaster Bomber ND622 attached to 57 Squadron based at East Kirkby. Lancaster Bomber ND622 was part of a force of 795 aircraft consisting of 572 Lancasters, 214 Halifaxes and 9 Mosquitoes despatched to attack the German city of Nuremberg on the

night of 30th March 1944. The main raid on Nuremberg ran into problems due to heavy cloud over the target area consequently little damage was done to the target.

95 aircraft were lost on this raid in total (66 Lancasters and 31 Halifaxes). Regretfully, the circumstances of how this aircraft met its fate are unknown. I can only presume that the aircraft exploded in mid-air as a result of enemy action, explaining why the remains of F/O Smart and Sgt Goddard were never found. These are remembered on the Runnymede Memorial. Sgt Marriott and Sgt Locke are buried in Bad Tolz (Durnbach) British Military Cemetery in plot 6 Row H Graves 1-2. The remaining three members of the crew were captured and became PoWs."

142447	F/Lt W E	Tickler	Pilot	RAF
152645	F/O R H	Smart	Navigator	RAF
1319846	Sgt A F	Goddard	Wop/Ag	RAF
185059	Sgt K R	Marriott	F/E	RAF
US10601395	T/Sgt W E	Steeper	Bomb Aimer	USAAF
1803629	Sgt A	Ferguson	M/U Gunner	RAF
1874060	Sgt R E	Locke	R/Gunner	RAF

Porthos, the third of the Musketeers to fall in battle.

It is perhaps necessary to explain about 'Combines'. Food in tins, once opened, had to be eaten the same day or it would be wasted as there was no way of keeping it fresh, especially in the hot weather. To overcome this it was obvious that sharing with one or two others was the answer.

This had the added benefit of being able to vary the choice of food, particularly if your combine received a mixture of food parcels from different countries. Combines ranged from just two men or in some cases up to eight or more. I was in one of four at this camp and we not only shared the food but also the 'duties' of preparing, cooking, washing up and scrounging extra food.

One very clear memory of a 'Combine' was the slicing of bread and dividing portions of food etc. To avoid any question of, '**His piece is bigger than mine**', we used playing cards. The duty cook would place a card on each slice or portion, say an Ace, King, Queen and Jack. Then similar cards were shuffled by another member of the combine and each would draw a card and take the slice or portion that matched that card. It might sound very childish but believe me, a man who had been in captivity two, three or more years and constantly hungry would quickly notice that his slice of bread, cake or biscuit was definitely .005 inches smaller than the other three.

It helped to pass the time and eliminated arguments about the size of a slice or portion. Non commissioned PoWs had no money, so an obvious alternative was the weekly issue of cigarettes. This was of great benefit to non-smokers who could always find a 'seller' who would part with his tin of salmon or corned beef for the established 'price' in cigarettes.

'Baiting' of the 'Goons' (German guards) was practised with care by taking spontaneous opportunities. For example, to stop a horse in Germany you rolled your tongue and made a brrrr noise. When an elderly Goon drove his even older looking horse and wooden cart down between the huts to collect rubbish, a head would pop out of a window just as he passed and, "Brrrrr" and the horse would stop. The Goon would start it going again only to have it stopped as he passed the next hut when another prisoner made the same noise.

Camaraderie was very noticeable despite the fact that with 60 men in one hut, or 2000 men in one compound, there were bound to be many differences of opinion. Arguments as well as close friendships formed. However, if it came to a confrontation with the Germans every single PoW would stand shoulder to shoulder with all the others.

One example of this was on a bright sunny day... an elderly German civilian carpenter was doing a repair of some sort out in the compound, he was sitting on the ground with a circle of PoWs watching him. He put his pliers down beside him and immediately a PoW on the other side asked him a question. As the carpenter turned his head to answer, a PoW this side reached down picked up the pliers and passed them to someone behind him.

When the German realised what had happened he began to rant and rave at all the innocent looking faces around him. Naturally, no one owned up and the poor German could not report the loss as he would be in trouble - tools were escape materials.

Opportunist ‘thefts’ of this sort went on all the time, be it food, timber, or any other material ‘that might come in useful’. They were frequently impromptu and backed up by any other prisoner who was about at that moment and could get in on the action.

19

THE RED SILK SCARF

This brings me nicely onto that scarf that I have mentioned a number of times. (You have been wondering about it, I'm quite sure.)

Every now and again we would be invaded by ferrets, not the furry kind, these walked on two legs, wore blue boiler suits and carried crowbars and torches. In a pack of about six or eight they would walk into the compound, go to a hut (randomly selected - I don't know?) and make everybody leave whilst they searched for escape materials, our 'Canary' (See page 124) or whatever. One day they picked our hut D7... all 60 of us were kicked out, then they began their search. Anything they found of a dubious nature they piled up on a table just inside the inner swing door. Jock McGregor was standing peeping through the door and called to me and said, "They have your red scarf, do you want it?" - Of course I said, "Yes." When all backs were turned, he reached in and grabbed it. He passed it to me and I popped round to Block B and gave it to Harry Bickell and went back to my hut.

The ferrets later discovered that it had been taken and were shouting and threatening everyone but to no avail. Fortunately, ferrets were not armed, so we were not in a life threatening situation. They kept us out of the hut for what seemed like two or three hours and yet not one single member of the hut moaned or suggested that I give the scarf back.

This was a typical 'battle' that had developed from a minor incident and in this instance with the full support of the prisoners of the hut. We had the upper hand for the ferrets could not report the 'theft' of the scarf as they themselves would be in serious trouble. We won a very strong moral victory as they had to depart with their 'loot', minus the scarf... but with their tails well and truly between their legs. (Do ferrets have tails?)

Another example of this form of gamesmanship that I witnessed at Heydekrug took place during a 'sheep count'. All prisoners were ushered into one half of the sports ground which was divided down the centre by a line of guards. A table and chairs were in a central gap. Prisoners were taken to the table five at a time, have their identity checked and then were ushered into the other half - like sheep. Whilst waiting, PoW No.1 started to play 'catch' with No.2. The ball was thrown back and forth a few times and then with a harder throw it went over the central line of guards. No.2 dashed through the line, picked up the ball and threw it back, following it back to 'his side' of the guards. This went on for some fifteen or twenty minutes with five or six overthrows. By this time the guards were bored and missed noticing that the 'catcher' did not return after throwing back the last ball, but another PoW immediately becoming the 'catcher' and the count was out by one man.

I never knew if this was an organised 'sting' (as they would call it today) or a totally impromptu happening. It does illustrate the fact that most PoWs would do anything for a bit of amusement or to 'bait' the Germans whenever they could.

The camp was so well organised that one could join various classes run by other PoWs who had particular skills, or you could be entertained by a 'speaker' visiting a hut to give a talk about a subject in which he was well versed. One that I remember was by a man who had been an undertaker, or had worked for a large London cemetery... gory to say the least.

There was also a camp theatre...one room had been

converted and the plays put on by capable prisoners were very popular. One night towards the end of summer there was a hullabaloo because the theatre was on fire. Cal Younger, one of the prisoners, wrote the following in his book **'No Flight From The Cage'** and I quote it here with his permission... as he knew far more about it than I did:

"Until the early hours of June ***13th**** *the cry of "Fire" had never been heard in the camp. Roused from sleep we heard feet scudding past the window. "All out. Fire. Fire." Terror first, the swelling nausea of terror. Then incredulity who would dare leave his barrack at this time of night? It was a still night; voices suddenly stirring across the compound seemed to be borne upon the stillness, seemed not to destroy it. From the scrummage of words only the insistent "Theatre. Fire. All out" could be distinguished. Barred doors. Pyjama clad figures fill the windows, and one at a time leap to the ground, emerging from the crush like pips squeezed from an orange. 'Buckets. Buckets.'*

We bring buckets. Someone's laundry, in soak, is poured over the floor. Along the length of the nine roomed barracks men in pyjamas and slippers are leaping, pausing, running. Flames we see gushing upward, jousting with each other, an angry ballet of leaping, cavorting, red dancers. The wooden built, tarred paper roofed theatre flares into a copper coated sky. But it is not of the theatre that we think now, it is of the nearby hut which houses the library, Dixie's office and sleeping quarters, and the store of nine million cigarettes, a quantity which had staggered the Gestapo.

But there was no breeze; the flames and the hurrying smoke spat and spurted straight up. To the consternation of the guards in the posten boxes, who did not know whether to fire at us or not, we formed bucket chains from the washhouse. German firemen stood gazing at the fire, trailing hoses that had a dry cleaned and pressed look about them.

All hands to the pumps. The buckets were filled, went from hand to hand. On the roof of the hut end-on to the burning theatre Ken Bowden and Jack Lipton stood precariously but carefree as ever. To them were passed the buckets, and they hurled the water, across the intervening fifteen feet, on to the flames which instantly vaporised it. More practically they kept dousing the end of the hut upon which they were mounted. At times they threw with, it seemed, wild inaccuracy, cheerfully apologising to the various German officers and NCO's upon whom the water descended. The twice soused Heinz must have had some doubts.

Suddenly the forgotten fire-hoses grew fat and water spouted from the nozzles. One jet hit a stout German officer between the eyebrows, and he fell flat on his back, gaped at by the man who held the hose and who, even now, did not think to direct the water elsewhere. The flames, dark flushed after the orgy, nosed along the ground, inquisitive and predatory, but there was little left for them to feed upon. Slowly they died. Gone was the theatre, built with skilful hands, employed with thoughtful purpose, with imagination, and unselfishness, in the cause of ameliorating unhappiness and boredom.

Next morning, in the ashes was recognisable only one thing a gramophone record, by some freak surviving, a record of "I don't want to set the world on fire", sung by Vera Lynn.

Strange and melancholy was the burnt, blank patch, the charred wood, the ashes. And though many said that the fire was the best show the theatre ever turned on, and perhaps it was, it is not the fire, not the drab burntness that we remember. Neat rows of seats made from Red Cross boxes, with eager prisoners leaning forward in them, the simple square proscenium, the atmosphere of first nights, Frank

Hunt's orchestra tuning up with the feast about to begin, the joyous cheering of success, the aisles packed as Peter Thomas, Mike Adams, Jack Connelly, Cyril Aynsley, Mike Custance, Alex Kerr, Dicky Beck, Mike Featherstone and so many others evoked the best in the art of debate.

There was that moving Watch Night service when, the darkened theatre become chapel, a single light burned in the shape of the Cross, while the choir sang softly, and one could single out the sweet, over-assured voices of the Welsh, and there was Shakespeare day when 5 former Oxford men and Cyril Aynsley each spoke on some aspect of the Bard's life and work.

Show business! How well Mr. W. Macqueen Pope would have written of the show business of the prison camp, recalling the delightful cameo of Lascelles's police sergeant in The Ringer, the tireless Peter Thomas in The Rotters, Grouse in June, and so many more, the courageous performances of the "leading ladies", Junior Booth, Roy Dotrice, Howard Squires and Alex Lewis among them, the versatile Bob Martin, Paddy Sheppard, the funny men, Snowball Morton, Bunny Austin, Ken Bowden and Jack Lipton, the bands of Fender and Parris, Tange Turnbull dancing, partnered by Ron Damman ...

The list grows too long perhaps. There were more shows, more men who will be remembered and some who probably are forgotten, who worked behind the scenes which John Murrell painted for every show. Backstage, where the electricians and the tailors worked, in a cupboard relocked by the Germans every time it was used, the amplifying set presented by the Swedish Y.M.C.A. had been kept.

The cause of the fire was generally believed to have been an electrical fault, some thought brought about by a model aircraft fouling a wire. Only a handful of prisoners knew that earlier that night the theatre had been broken into, the cupboard forced open, and equipment which it was imperative to have to keep the radio working, removed.

And, to prevent the crime being discovered for its motive was palpable-an ingenious time-bomb was set by its maker, Bristow. The theatre, which would soon have played its last show, in any case, was destroyed, but the voice of the canary was assured."

The 'Canary' was the secret radio from which we received the BBC news broadcasts. These were relayed to each hut by trusted prisoners who went from hut to hut to read out the latest bulletins. It was built from stolen and hand made parts by Eric Bristow and survived numerous searches.

In the next few weeks rumours abounded as the Russian Army advanced, and on July **13th*** it was announced that we were to abandon the camp. Those in the American compound were moved first followed by 'K' Lager and then gradually our lager, starting with A block. Those of us in D block, being the last, had the pickings of all that had been abandoned but there was little time to unpack and repack, so we too abandoned them.

On the day it was announced that we were moving I was approached by a Canadian who had been a PoW for some 2 or 3 years. Knowing that I was relatively new he asked if I would carry some cigarettes for him as he had a large stock, the deal was that I could keep half of what I managed to get to the next camp. As cigarettes were `money' and I did not have many anyway, I agreed to carry a quantity (I think it was 3 or 4,000 packed into a kitbag that I had scrounged). I kept my word but with many thousands of them being abandoned when the move took place I could have kept all that I could carry.

20

STALAG 357
THORN & FALLINGBOSTEL

The next journey in the cattle trucks was the worst ever. The area between the pairs of sliding doors was again partitioned off with barbed wire, leaving the small area either side to accommodate 30 men in each. The very hot weather made it extremely uncomfortable. Fortunately it was only a two day journey and we thankfully disembarked at the railway sidings at Thorn in Poland and were marched through the darkened streets to a camp not too far distant from the town. This was Stalag 357, our new home.

My Canadian friend collected his cigarettes, leaving me with just about 2000, the equivalent of about 9 months at 50 per week plus the weekly issue whilst supplies were available. These would prove to be godsend in the coming months.

We learned later that we had been fortunate as the prisoners of the other two lagers, almost 4000 men, had been sent by sea and had been locked in the hold for some 60 or more hours. Despite the heat they were given little or no water and nothing at all to eat. One wonders who gave that order... did he think that prisoners would find ways of escaping many miles off shore in the Baltic Sea?

When they eventually reached land they were taken by train to Tychow and then, handcuffed in pairs, were forced to run all the way to the camp by Kriegsmarine Cadets with fixed bayonets... which they used to prod any stragglers.

Our new camp had smaller wooden huts and ours was quite close to the wire fence, beyond which was the road into town. On Sundays, people from the town would walk up past the camp including many girls who were a sight for sore eyes.

It is believed that some of the Polish prisoners had relatives in the area. Our stay here was only a temporary stop as just under a month later we were on the move again. This time, again in overcrowded cattle trucks, right across northern Germany to Fallingbostel near Celle and not that many miles from Hanover. Not as good a camp as Heydekrug and as the war progressed and transportation became difficult, food shortages began to take effect.

On arrival we were moved into empty barracks and I was fortunate to get into the far corner of a hut close to a window. By coincidence, also in this same corner was 'Hugo' Hughes, Canadian bomb aimer in Bill Dykes' crew. We formed a two man combine adding a few others over the next few weeks to eke out the joint rations as efficiently as possible.

It was at this camp that the Germans, having heard that German PoWs in North Africa had no beds or books, decided to remove all our straw palliasses, half our bed boards and close our library. Word soon spread and lots of books were removed from the library before it was locked. As for the beds, most made hammocks from blankets and slept quite comfortably for the six to eight weeks that this episode lasted.

Cooking facilities here were almost nonexistent. Ingenuity born out of necessity brought about 'The Blower'... a simple device consisting of a large and small pulley wheel mounted on a plank (usually a bed board) and connected by a length of string. (See photos opposite page). A handle on the large pulley drove the small pulley at high speed which spun a fan made from a food tin lid, forcing air up through a very small amount of fuel (wood chips etc) that would boil water within a very short time. 'Tin Bashing' was an art that many acquired, turning food tins into drinking mugs, plates, dishes etc.

This skill, when devoted to a 'Blower', produced some

These pictures of what appears to be a post war reconstruction of a blower (too well built to have been an original !!!) clearly illustrate the principle. Photos by Alan Parr taken at RAF Cosford Museum and reproduced with their kind approval.

extremely efficient devices. Inevitably, bets were soon made on the fastest to boil a given measure of water. The Klim tin (Powdered milk tin) was particularly useful in that it had a lid that fitted on the 'stepped' open end. These made mugs with lids to keep the flies from the 'brew'. They also made fine storage containers for 'bits and pieces' such as needles, thread and spare buttons for example. However, the Klim tin had much more important uses. By removing the bottom, the recessed end of a second tin would fit snugly into it, then another into the bottom of that and so on - eventually you have a pipe - used in tunnels to send fresh air to the tunnel face.

A consignment of Red Cross parcels arrived just before Christmas...but not enough to go round so these had to be shared. I think it was one parcel between five men. In view of the recent weeks on low rations these made a real Christmas treat but we were now aware of the dangers of over indulging.

Shortage of fuel resulted in a number of prisoners signing Temporary Parole (Limited to 24 hours. We had been told during training that we were not allowed to sign 'Permanent Parole'. This could be construed as 'siding with the enemy' and traitorous). In groups of twelve with one guard we were allowed out of the camp to collect whatever we could carry from the nearby woods. I did go out on one party and it was most pleasurable to be outside the wire looking in, even for an hour or two. The cold winter, shortage of food and fuel seemed to drag on and on. The only thing that kept us going was the 'Canary' still singing, bringing us the news of the advances that the allies were making.

January and February 1945 were the worst period ever... little fuel or food, cold wet dismal days, no wonder many took to their bunks and only appeared for 'Appel' and when food was dished out.

21

THE SHORT WALK

Then in March 1945, those of us who were fit enough were told that we were to leave camp and to take only what we could carry. It seemed that we were going on foot to an unknown destination... and future. Much packing and unpacking followed but essentially we included whatever food we had, any extra clothing, particularly woollen items and other bartering materials, namely, cigarettes and small tins of coffee. I had just under 800 cigarettes when we left camp.

In groups of about 500, with a number of guards to each group, we left camp and walked in a north easterly direction using country roads in most cases. Where possible we slept in barns, but on two occasions we had to sleep in the open.

We had a sprinkling of American airmen in our column and I joined two of them to form a small combine. One spoke quite good German which came in very useful when we passed through a village or stopped at a farm.

During this 'march' across Germany we bartered our (my) cigarettes and woollen clothing for food and stole whatever food we could, including a forty pound suckling pig. In the darkness at the farm at which we had stopped I found the pig sty and a Canadian, using a brick, killed the piglet. He and I carried it all the next day in a sack hanging on an eight foot by two inch diameter bamboo pole. I have often wondered how, in the darkness, we found the sack and bamboo pole. He joined our combine and that night we borrowed a 'Witch's Cauldron' that another forward thinking PoW had carried over his shoulder from the camp. He never had to scrounge or barter for food as his 'cauldron' was in great demand by the others who had no way of cooking the potatoes or swedes that they had begged, borrowed or stolen during the day's march. The piglet was cut up, boiled in salty water until tender and divided up that evening. We gave some to the guard who had been with us most of the time as he was on short rations.

A day or two later this guard took a great risk in allowing the German speaking American to leave the column and go to a nearby farm to barter for food. The rest of the combine stayed close to the guard as 'voluntary hostages'. The exercise was successful and we shared the bread and eggs with him.

We slept in the open one very cold night on what I believe was a football pitch just outside a village. There was a severe frost and in the morning one of my feet was frozen. The Canadian removed my shoe and sock, helped me hobble over to a nearby stream and told me to put my foot in the water. Amazingly, as there was no feeling in my foot it did not feel cold, but gradually, as it thawed out so the pain started.

It was excruciating but eventually it eased and then I could feel the cold water as it coursed over my bare foot. Apparently this was a common method used in northern Canada to avoid frost bite. I was able to walk as normal when we moved off again. We passed through Lunenburg, then Lauenburg... in one of these two places we had to pass over a road bridge to cross the river. As we waited on one bank for a convoy of lorries to cross, many of us took the opportunity to bathe in the cold water.

This was the first real wash for many days and although very cold it was good to feel clean all over. We eventually crossed and struggled on until we reached the village of Kittlitz. This was 35 days after leaving Fallingbostel and it would have been around the 5th May 1945.

The Germans then decided that there was no point in going further as we would be getting nearer the Russians than we were to the British. The next afternoon some of the guards disappeared and the few who remained handed over their rifles and became our prisoners. **We were free... well almost.**

Most of us were in khaki as our original uniforms were replaced with captured army ones when ours wore out. The Germans never captured much in the way of RAF equipment but had large army stocks that were left behind at Dunkirk and possibly some from the Middle East.

I think it was the morning of May 8th 1945 that a British Army reconnaissance jeep drove into Kittlitz, the occupants were surprised to find that the 'army' was already there. They were soon put in the picture and we were officially 'released.' I say released in quotes as we were told to stay there until transport arrived to take us back.

I had some friends in the group behind ours and the reconnaissance jeep driver told me that they were just a couple of miles down the lane in the next village. I decided to walk down to see how they were. Leaving the farm I strolled down the country lane and after about half a mile I rounded a bend and coming towards me was a troop of about 30 German soldiers, lead by an officer on horseback. I stopped in the middle of the road wondering what to do next, when the officer called out to me in broken English, asking where my Commanding Officer was as he wished to surrender.

Breathing more easily, I promptly replied that he was in the village just up the road behind me. I then told him that no transport was allowed and he would have to dismount and also hand over weapons. He got off his horse, handed me the reins and his 32 calibre William Tell Mark 2 revolver. He then instructed his men to stack their rifles at the side of the road and with a smart salute he marched them away to find 'My Commanding Officer', obviously thinking that I was one of the fighting troops who had taken over this area.

I had never ridden a horse in my life... I failed at least three attempts to get on it, each time I put my foot in the stirrup the horse moved away from me. I ended up climbing on a fence and stepping over the saddle in a quick scramble. The horse started to canter and I hung on with arms round its neck as my feet tried to find the stirrups. I used the only way I knew of stopping a German horse. I shouted, “BRRRRRR”, loudly and it stopped, nearly throwing me off its back.

I managed to get my feet into the stirrups and settled firmly in the saddle, clutching the reins. I got the horse to walk slowly back to the farm (The officer and his soldiers would have been long gone by now as at least half an hour had passed). As I approached the field next to the barn, the horse began to speed up into a canter and I once again shouted, “BRRRRR”, and almost went over its head as it instantly stopped. There was a cheer from some other kriegies (Kriegesgefangenen - prisoner of war) who were in the field and who were amused at my comical attempt at riding. An Aussie came over and helped me to dismount. He then climbed on and galloped round the field doing all the ‘cowboy’ tricks as he enjoyed his first ride for a number years.

It was ‘my’ trophy but there was no way that I could get it back behind the lines let alone get it home so I presented it to the farmer in whose barn we were sleeping. It transpired that he had been a cavalry officer in the First World War. It gave him great pleasure to mount the horse, and using a broom handle as a sword he went through all the standard drill that a cavalry officer would do.

This ‘gift’ resulted in the farmer killing a pig. I assume it was cooked as I don’t recall eating any. I only remember seeing the pig hanging head down from a beam as he gutted it.

There was a main road nearby and we spent some happy hours lined up on both sides selecting German soldiers or smartly attired civilians to stop to be searched. Though fully equipped when entering the line, many had nothing left by the time they reached the end. Some were even minus a belt for their trousers... well, could you blame us?

After waiting for transport for two days or more we took matters into our own hands and a small group of us commandeered a ration lorry and started to drive to the west.

Around midday we pulled into a village where British tanks and lorries where stationary around the village green. We stopped and some of the soldiers came over to chat to us, offering mugs of hot sweet tea and cigarettes. One climbed into the back of 'our vehicle' and looked to see what was there. He shouted to a mate to bring over a hand axe and using it he broke open the top of a large barrel. It was full of Schnapps and within minutes there was a crowd of soldiers, with their tin mugs, buzzing around the barrel like flies round some rotten meat. When we finally departed we got a good send off from the non too sober squaddies.

At Lauenburg the Red Caps (Military Police) were only allowing one way traffic and we had to abandon the ration lorry and walk over the bridge. In the town another Red Cap told us where there was a car park where we might find another vehicle. A few of our group went to look whilst the rest of us split up to search elsewhere, all arranging to meet in the car park later. Why I went out on my own I have no idea but as it was I found a brand new DUKW on a garage forecourt with the keys in the side pocket of the door. I managed to start the engine but that was all, I could not work out how to get it into gear, putting the keys back where I found them (stupid thing to do) I went in search of the group. I found one who was a driver but when we got back to the garage the DUKW had gone, probably stolen by another kriegie. We went to the rendezvous at the car park and met up with the others who had found a working canvas tilt truck with bench seats down each side. They had already refuelled it from other vehicles and off we set towards Lunenburg. Just outside the town, on a country road, were two young girls about fifteen or sixteen years old. They were thumbing a lift... as we had room we stopped and they climbed onboard.

They were 'displaced persons' from the Baltic coast area and were trying to get over the Elbe into the British sector. It was well established that east of the Elbe would be under Russian control. We all agreed that we should try and help them and as we approached Lunenburg we hid the two girls by means of them laying flat on our laps and us covering them with blankets. It was just as well as we were stopped by Red Caps who opened the back to look at us. Satisfied, they directed us to a side road which lead to some barracks where we could stay the night. One also told us that transport would be there in the morning to take us to the airfield from where we would be flown home.

We drove down the road, went straight past the main entrance gate to the barracks and drove a couple of miles further on until we came to a forest area. Here we helped the girls out, gave them provisions and cigarettes to barter with and wished them good luck. I have often wondered what became of them. We then drove back up to the barracks.

The rooms were full of kriegies of all ranks and services, there were even some Royal Navy... but the majority were RAF and Army.

We ate our first meal as 'free' men in the canteen, served up by the army cooks and whilst I cannot remember what we ate I am sure that we enjoyed it.

Next morning we were all bundled into trucks and some buses and were driven up to the northern Dutch border and disembarked at an airfield near Emden. We were assembled and told that aircraft were flying back and forth all day and it was just a question of being patient as our turn would come. Meanwhile, as we waited we had the opportunity of chatting to some of the troops. I will never forget the laughter that followed after one soldier walked past me carrying a tray of sliced bread... with my kriegie training and sleight of hand I soon relieved him of a couple of slices without his knowledge. Eaten dry, it tasted like sponge cake and together with the kriegie next to me we ate it with huge grins on our faces.

Ted with his 'captured' booty that the 'squaddie' never knew had been 'rescued' - a trick well learned during captivity. (Sketch by John Ward)

22

'GOOD OLD BLIGHTY'

Eventually it was our turn to move up to be next in line. The men ahead of us boarded a Dakota - the next aircraft to taxi into the boarding area was a Lancaster, not a 49 Squadron one, that would have been too much of a coincidence, but nevertheless a Lancaster. To me, this was a very fitting way to return to good old blighty.

It was quite a short flight, landing at Dunsfold in Surrey. The aircraft taxied right along the perimeter to a point near the control tower and we began to disembark. Nearly every ex-prisoner knelt and kissed the turf as soon as his feet touched the ground.

We were then grabbed by two WAAFs who kissed us and walked us up to the delousing tent where operators pumped white powder up our trouser legs, sleeves and down our neck and waist. They then waited for us to appear at the other end. We were then lead up into the hanger where the WVS, WI, Red Cross and many other female volunteers, with tears running down their cheeks, handed us a cup of tea and a slice of cake. It was so emotional but I guess we were so overwhelmed with our feelings of actually being home and the war being over… it was hard to take it all in.

My two WAAFs then whisked me off to the stores where I was issued with a complete new uniform with all the accessories. Then into a barrack block where I went into the shower and clearly recall the wonderful feeling of an unlimited supply of hot water pouring down on me ... I could have stayed there much longer but naturally, there was a queue of men waiting so five minutes was the limit.

My 'escorts' had meanwhile sown on my stripes and brevets, inserted the crown above the stripes and they 'being very proper' stood outside the door whilst I dressed.

I have no real memories of what happened next, I know I telephoned my home and spoke to my young brother David. The next thing I was on a train full of ex-kriegies on our way to RAF Cosford. As the train passed through north west London I could have jumped out and walked home except the train was going rather fast.

On arrival at Cosford the scene, in what I believe was a hangar, could be likened to a modern airport with queues alongside queues all leading up to tables. Here intelligence officers interrogated each prisoner establishing who they were. We understood that this was necessary as many misplaced persons and even some Germans were attempting to get away from the continent using stolen documents. Every ex-prisoner, when identity was confirmed, had his details entered on a large two page form which they then signed. (These forms provided some useful information in later years).

I am not sure how long we were at Cosford, probably just one day, but that part is another blank. I was then on the train back to London complete with kitbag, I changed stations and caught the tube train to my home at Rayners Lane. I left the heavy kitbag with the station ticket collector to collect later.

As I walked down my home avenue, a neighbour, the first to greet me, rushed over the road gave me a welcome home kiss and handed me a paper bag that contained a chunk of cheese (probably a week's ration for herself and her husband).

I went straight to my bedroom when I got indoors and just laid back on the bed as I gathered my thoughts and realised how lucky I had been to have survived and having to mentally slap myself to believe that it was true. **I WAS HOME**.

As one would expect, we all went to the local pub that night. I had a pint of mild and bitter which lasted me all evening. I left half a pint in the glass when it came time for us to walk back home (With careful training, it did not take very long to get back to being able to imbibe a whole pint).

Only a few days later a parcel arrived with various dates and place stamps showing it had been returned as undelivered via Lisbon. It was one of the parcels sent to me via the Red Cross by my parents. They were allowed to send (I believe) two each year. These usually contained pyjamas, underwear, socks, books, chocolate and other bits and bobs that would be needed in a PoW camp. We felt that our 'ship had come home' when one arrived. In the whole of the 17 months I was there I only ever received one such parcel.

On opening it, two books fell out, the first one was 'How To Cook Fish From The World' or some such title, the second (which I still have to this day) was a 900 page pre-war 'Mrs Beeton's Cookery Book' with numerous colour pages of delectable dishes and recipes - take the yolks of 12 eggs - VERY useful in a PoW Camp! I could have charged a couple of cigarettes a time to look at the pictures... and drool.

I looked up my friend Doreen, but she was working in London and often stayed with friends rather than travel back and forth each day. I also met up with Freda (Peggy) and although she was at work during the day, her father, Jack, was home on leave. We spent some time chatting and getting to know one another. Peggy and I started seeing a lot of each other and within four months we were married.

This turned out to be a big mistake. As was quite natural for the few months after the war ended, all servicemen, particularly those who had seen active service, were feted at almost every turn especially when in uniform, which in my case was all the time as my civilian clothes were too small for me now. I could never buy a round of drinks, pay to go to the cinema or even for a taxi ride in London. I regret that Peggy became carried away thinking that she was in love with me when in fact she was in love with the aura of 'hero worship' that was created.

I had got a posting to the Princess Mary Hospital at RAF Halton which was only 35 minutes from home by train. We managed to rent half a house and began to make it into our home. The Catering Officer had advised me that there was a permanent vacancy for a Warrant Officer (Catering) and hinted that she would like me in the post. We discussed it and I confirmed that I might stay in the RAF as a 'Regular' as I thought this was a very good opportunity.

I should explain that all aircrew ranks were temporary and taking up another 'trade' would mean reverting to the lowest rank of AC2 in that trade but still retaining the aircrew rank and rate of pay. A temporary arrangement that was necessary to deal with all the ex prisoners of war.

Being so close to home it would almost be like working in 'Civvie street'. In a few weeks I was posted to RAF Beaulieu in the New Forest as a Corporal Hospital Cook and had my own private billet in half a Nissen hut on the edge of the forest and some way from the actual airfield. A few months later I was posted as a Sergeant Hospital Cook (but I was still also a Warrant Officer) to RAF Creden Hill in Herefordshire.

I had not taken much leave in those few months but had managed a few weekends. It was a huge shock when I got a letter from Peggy asking me to return the key as she had moved out and gone back to live with her mother (In the prison camps this would have been called a 'Dear John' letter, many of which were received from unfaithful wives).

I was completely shattered by this and got an emergency 48 hours leave to see if I could sort it out. On the doorstep of her mother's flat (I was not even invited in) she told me the marriage was over, no explanation, no reasons, no apologies, just that she had made a mistake.

I collected my personal belongings and headed back to camp. The next few months or so are rather blurred as I began to drink heavily. I had taken this posting at the hospital for two reasons, it would be near to home and I was back into catering and hoped it would become my future trade. Despite many attempts to repair the break up of my marriage I had no success, I never found out the real reason that it failed.

With a complete change in my plans for the future I opted to go back on flying if I could. After enquiring I found that there was a new recruitment scheme for three years permanent service and four years on the reserves. They offered a £25 'bounty' when signing on and £175 at the end of the three years. It doesn't sound much these days but back then in 1946 it was very attractive. The small snag was you had to have left the service then rejoin (or so I was lead to believe).

The date for my demobilisation had passed a few months previously. I had not bothered to take it as the Catering Officer was quite happy to keep me on and I was quickly being promoted in my 'new trade'.

I approached the WAAF clerk in the orderly room and said,

"Can I have my demob please?"

"When is it due", asked the clerk?

"About two months ago", I replied.

To say she looked surprised would be putting it mildly when you consider most conscripts and volunteers could not get out of the service fast enough.

23

DEMOB & RE-ENLISMENT

On the 22nd July 1946 I left Creden Hill and travelled home, reporting the next morning to RAF Uxbridge to complete my discharge. When all the papers had been prepared and the amount of pay that I was due had been calculated, I was about to sign when the clerk noticed that I was an ex-prisoner of war. He asked if I had any German money or Lager Geld (Prison camp money for officers only) that I needed to exchange.

I then remembered I had a 100 Rentenmark note that was one of a large number in an envelope that I took from a well dressed German when we were searching them the day after the war ended. A British soldier who was with me said they were worthless so I kept one and threw the rest into a ditch. The clerk looked up a list and handed me another £3 and some silver - there must have been at least a 100 notes in that envelope that I threw in the ditch, maybe that British soldier knew but was not saying.

Leaving Uxbridge later that morning I travelled up to Wembley where I was issued with a demob suit and other civilian clothing. I then caught the tube train back to my home where I dressed up in civilian clothes legally for the first time in 5 years. (You were not supposed to wear them when home on leave during war time).

Later, feeling very conspicuous, I made my way to the tube station, meeting my mother half way. I remember giving her the 'pork pie' style hat that I was wearing as I did not feel comfortable in it. I caught a tube straight up to Kingsway, walked to the Air Ministry and into the recruitment office.

I asked if I could to sign on for the 3 year scheme. The clerk began to fill in the application and after name, rank and number etc asked:-

"When were you discharged?"

"This morning", I replied.

The form completed it was taken to another office, reappearing in the hand of a Squadron Leader who smiled and jokingly said…

"Didn't you like Civvie Street?"

With all the preliminaries completed I was sent on my way and told that I would be called back into uniform in due course. I was already on paid demob leave (I think it was 4 weeks) and could still wear uniform if I wished. It was during that short period that I met up with Doreen again. She was now working for the BBC as one of the cast in the Monday Night at Eight radio programme. She was staying with her mother for a few days and invited me to join her on the Friday for a mystery evening out. Dressed in my almost new Warrant Officer's uniform, with a few medal ribbons, we met up as arranged and travelled by bus to Bentley Priory in Stanmore.

This was Fighter Command Headquarters and the Control Centre during the war. We entered the gates... she showed a pass and we were directed to this large building which had been set up with row upon row of seats facing a stage. The room was almost full and bold as brass she took my arm and walked me to the front where two reserved seats awaited us.

Many a curious glance was given as this Warrant Officer, with a most attractive young lady on his arm, sat amongst all the gold braid of the Senior Officers. The lights dimmed, the curtains parted and there was the RAF Dance Orchestra (I am not sure if it was The Sky Rockets or the Squadronaires).

Doreen had sung with one of the bands and knew some of the players in the other band. We were entertained for a while with popular music then at the interval Doreen stood up and I followed her to the door beside the stage. We then had a very pleasant 15 minutes drinking with the band as Doreen introduced me. On our return we were facing the entire audience as we crossed the floor to regain our seats and again were met by many curious and I believe many envious glances. Doreen later married Paul Fenouhlet, leader of the BBC Light Orchestra.

By this time, both my brothers had been demobbed and I spent the next couple of months doing odd jobs pending my second 'call up'. This duly arrived at the end of September and on November 4th 1946 I reported to Burtonwood in Lancashire where I was inducted with about 1100 other men who had also re-joined... approximately 75% of us were ex-PoWs.

New ranks for aircrew were introduced around this time to replace the temporary war time ones. I became a Signaller IIB, the equivalent of a Sergeant, but as the new badges of rank were not available we continued to wear our previous rank which in my case was a Warrant Officer. In addition, at some training bases they even created aircrew messes which separated us from the ground staff. There had been instances of bad feelings from some ground staff who may have served some 15 years before reaching the rank of Sergeant whereas aircrew might do this in 2 years.

On the first day we were paid our £25 gratuity and we played cards all afternoon, some winning heavily and others losing it all. The card school of about ten players decided to go out on the town with the winners paying for the losers. We took two taxis into St Helens where we went to a fairly large hotel. We were given a large table in the centre of the restaurant and began to enjoy the evening. Cigarettes were still in short supply and, as I had run out, I went downstairs to the reception office and enquired if they had any. They did but only Players Escudo's, the most expensive brand.

These were in a box of 200. I bought it and returned to the table placing it in the middle for anyone to help themselves. After a while an elderly gentleman came over and asked me if he could possibly buy a few as he and his guests had also run out. Feeling magnanimous (or maybe a little tiddly) I gave him about twenty and said, "Have these on us"... he thanked me and returned to his table. When we had finished our meal we were discussing what to do next when the gentleman returned and enquired what were our plans for the evening. Having none, he explained that there was private ball upstairs for members of the brewery trade and invited us to join him as his guests, adding that the bar was free - we needed no further encouragement and followed his party to the ball. It was an extremely pleasant event and went on until the early hours of the morning by which time we were in a very merry mood. We thanked all and sundry, kissed as many ladies as we could, and took taxis back to camp.

Over the next few months we were shunted via South Cerney in Gloucestershire to Weston Super Mare, back to South Cerney, then to Ballykelly in Northern Ireland. Back again to South Cerney and then finally, those of us who were Wop/Ag's went to RAF Swanton Morley, near East Dereham in Norfolk, the wireless school for our refresher course.

The date was the 21st Jan 1947. Some four weeks later we were snowed in - fuel and food could not get through to the camp so we carried our necessary kit and trudged through the thick snow for some five miles to East Dereham. Here we caught whatever trains were able to get through and went to our respective destinations (home).

A friend, Dickie, who lived near Hereford was not sure how far he would get so I arranged that he could come back to my home if he was unable to get through. The following afternoon he arrived, very tired and very scruffy having slept in the station waiting room all night, so it was a quick bath and into bed for him. We had to go to Uxbridge each week to draw pay but were pleased to find that we got an extra amount as it was classed as 'Survival Leave'. This lasted for some six weeks and on returning to Swanton Morley we had to cope with the flooding caused by the huge amount of melting snow.

The refresher course brought me up-to-date with the various changes in wireless procedures and for the second time I was posted to Swinderby. Here I crewed up with ex flying boat pilot, Wing Commander Arney and navigator, Sgt Don See. We flew Wellingtons as we welded together, with an anticipated posting to Coastal Command at Lossimouth where the skipper was to be the Commanding Officer.

An incident occurred on this course which resulted in an uncomfortable flight on one cross country exercise. The fuel filler cover on the starboard wing was secured by a spring loaded turnscrew which suddenly gave way and the cover lifted like a flap. This caused so much drag that the skipper had trouble holding the aircraft straight and level due to the strain on his wrists. He called me up into the cockpit (which was dual controlled) and I took half the strain and in this fashion we flew back to base making a safe if somewhat shaky landing.

There was a surplus of Wellington aircraft and we frequently had the pleasure of being transported in another Wimpy to Little Rissington, a Maintenance Unit (M.U.) in Oxfordshire, to collect BRAND NEW aircraft that had been mothballed. The flying hours were chalked on the tyre and was usually around three hours. Once we were airborne, the skipper would let me fly it back to base and in clear weather I did this by following the A1 trunk road up to Newark and then turning right up the Fosseway (A46) to Swinderby airfield. These aircraft would be flown until their first major overhaul was due, then towed just across the road to a hanger type building where they would be scrapped.

At the end of the course the skipper apologised to Don and me that we would not be going with him as they already had a surplus of wireless operators and navigators at Lossiemouth. He told us that he had arranged for us to be transferred to Transport Command and to report to No. 1382 T.I.C.U. at RAF Wymeswold following ten days leave.

During this leave I spent some time meeting up with my old crowd. On Whit Sunday lunch time we were having a few social drinks and one of them, Sid Bedborough, was chatting to an attractive young lady who was sitting at the bar with an elderly gentleman at her side (Her father as I later discovered). I joined into the conversation and after some ten minutes asked Sid if he was ever going to introduce me to the young lady to whom I was very attracted... his reply was,

“This is Betty, I thought everybody knew Betty”.

I eventually managed to get a stool, sat beside her and we chatted for some time like old friends and I began to think she liked my company. I wasted no time and asked her for a date which was readily accepted. We spent the whole of Whit Monday together which we both enjoyed and I hoped that this was the beginning of a relationship.

We saw each other almost every day until my leave ended and became very attracted to each other. With promises to write when I packed and departed once again, I had no real idea what was ahead, but I guess that was part of the ’adventure’ phase that I was still going through.

Photo Page 1

Betty Wilcox with life time friend Dot Everett (49 Sqdn M T Driver) outside the Petwood Hotel, Woodhall Spa at the 49 Squadron Reunion.

On the night of January 2nd /3rd 1944 when I got out to the aircraft I still had my wallet in my pocket. As we never took anything that might provide information to the enemy, I handed it to Dot for safe keeping. The following morning it was confirmed that we were 'missing'. When Dot mentioned it to Betty she was told of my three dreams of being a PoW. The next day Dot rang my father to tell him she had my wallet and mentioned my dreams, this was misinterpreted as being some unofficial 'leaked' information and my parents were thus convinced I was already safe in a prison camp. Later, after the Red Cross notification that I was in fact a PoW came through, Dot and Betty accepted an invitation to spend a few days with my parents and my wallet was delivered at the same time.

PoWs boarding a Lancaster for the journey home. Photo from one of the WAAFs who was there at the time. (Name withheld on request)
The Lancaster is from 463 RAAF Squadron from Waddington.

Photo Page 2

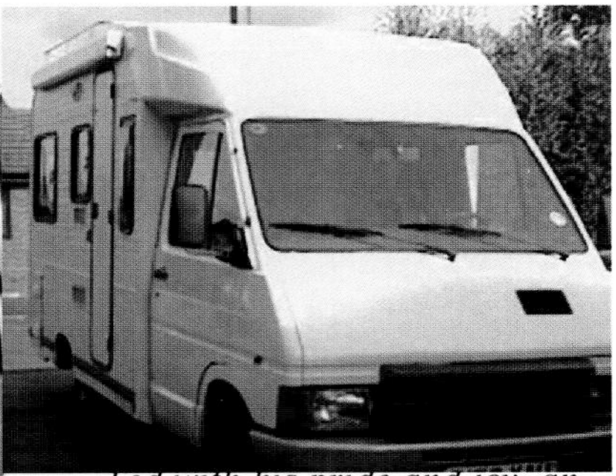

Ted with his pride and joy, an ancient motorhome that he has lovingly refurbished and updated over a three year period.

Ted in a Queen's flight A125 from RAF Northolt. Pilot G/Capt John Maas.

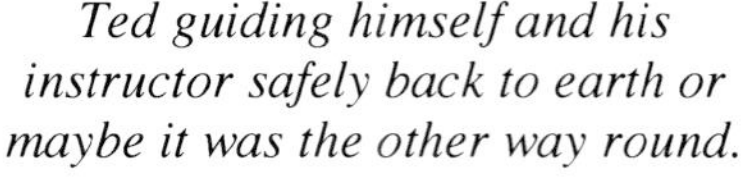

Ted guiding himself and his instructor safely back to earth or maybe it was the other way round.

(left). Ted at the Imperial War Museum on the press day for the launch of the Great Escapers Exhibition. After the TV shoot, we were surrounded by school children in red sweatshirts asking questions. S/Ldr Laidlow-Petersen, in our party, described the scene as 'Distinguished Gentlemen in a field of poppies'.

Photo Page 3

Ted and Jackie after their charity parachute jump in 1996

Tony on his wedding day

Four generations of the Cachart family
Ted, Jackie and Tony (top row)
Hayley (left)
Lucy (right)
Edward (bottom left)
Emily (bottom right)
and Megan (centre)

Photo Page 4

Betty Lowrie who I met on Whit Sunday 1947.
We married on August 31st 1952.
Betty died on 18th July 1991.

Photo Page 5

F/Sgt Ted on his 20th birthday in June 1945 - just four weeks after being released as a prisoner of war in Germany. The jacket has crocodile clips on the back to take in the slack. Note the VERY new stripes. His promotion to Warrant Officer was promulgated on July 19th 1945

Photo Page 6

Nancy Pants Last Flight - by John Ward depicting the crew preparing to board her for the last time.

24

TRANSPORT COMMAND

So, another change in direction and a new challenge. I duly reported in to 1382 TCU RAF Wymeswold. After some preliminaries I was crewed up with pilot, Flying Officer 'Duke' Baker and navigator, Warrant Officer Bob O'Connel, both Canadians who had served in the RCAF and had signed on in the RAF for a short term of regular service.

We were a three man crew on Dakotas and I was to be both signaller and second pilot. (No take offs or landings). Our first flight together was on the **13th*** November 1947. Then, having just about settled in at this base on December 10th the Unit transferred to North Luffenham. For the first time we moved ourselves by air, taking off from RAF Wymeswold with all our kit on board and landing at RAF North Luffenham.

My new crew F/O 'Duke' Baker (Pilot)   W/O Bob O'Connel, (Navigator)
Both Ex - RCAF

Then on February 20th, the training in handling the aircraft and the requisite number of day and night cross country exercises completed, we transferred to No. 1333 T.S.T.U at RAF Netheravon. Here we learned to tow Horsa gliders, drop panniers (some low level without parachutes) and last but not least, trainee paratroops of the Parachute Regiment.

I had a two week attachment to Upper Heyford for a course as Jump Master (the man who 'helped' the paratroops out of the door). I was supposed to do two parachute jumps, one from a static balloon and one from the Dakota but the wind speeds were something like 20 mph and it was considered too dangerous (when we baled out over Germany the winds were around 80 mph). Maybe they took that jump into consideration as I still passed the course.

On rejoining the crew at Netheravon we completed our training and were then told we had been posted to Kabrit in Egypt and were sent home on 4 weeks embarkation leave. This was between the middle of March and April 1948.

Betty and I were now courting and this posting was the last thing we wanted but 'orders are orders'. We made the most of our time together and the leave seemed to pass very quickly but the time came to depart and I met Duke in London and we caught the train to Lyneham. From here we would fly as passengers in a Transport Command York to Egypt via Malta.

The British Government were selling off all sorts of surplus aircraft at that time. These were bought by various countries at what I believed were ridiculously low prices (£10 for a Spitfire). They were even delivering them! Our navigator, Bob, had been commandeered as the second of a two man crew to deliver a Mosquito to Greece. He would then fly in a civil aircraft to El Hamra and meet us there.

25

COASTAL COMMAND

On arrival at Middle East HQ at El Hamra we met up with Bob and were then interviewed by the A.O.C who first of all said that he did not recognise the new aircrew ranks in his command and told Bob and me to replace them with our original ranks. He then commented on the fact that all three of us had previously been on Lancasters and wondered if we would like to transfer back onto to them.

A quick conference and we agreed. He then said we would be flown back to Malta to join 37 Squadron on Coastal Command. Fourteen days later we flew back to Malta and we were in Ramit David in Palestine ten days after that. Owing to the internal fighting between the Jews and Arabs we were confined to the camp other than when we flew.

In the photograph on page 156 I am wearing a white silk scarf. This was a gift from my brother Bob when he learned that my 'lucky' red one had been thrown away by Peggy.

As one can imagine, a metal fuselage sitting in the sun gets very hot. A Wop/Ag's daily task was to change the small accumulator that provided power for the intercom system. To avoid the heat we did this around 0700 hours and each Wop would do two aircraft on alternate days.

One morning when it was my turn I cycled down and collected two accumulators, rode out to the line of aircraft and parked my bike at the rear of the first, unlocked the door, climbed in and changed the accumulator. I then climbed out and locked the door, then ducked under the fuselage and went into the second plane and repeated the operation. As I climbed out I was collared by two SP's who, despite my protestations, bundled me into a Jeep and drove me to the guardroom.

Some quick checks were made and a mild apology given with a warning about wearing the white scarf - it was a standard form of identification by one of the terrorist gangs and I had been seen acting suspiciously by doing something to

Ted with various 37 Squadron aircrew but regretfully names are not listed.

A 37 Squadron Lancaster
Note the top turret has been removed.

the door of one aircraft, then dodging under the fuselage and getting into the other.

On two occasions we flew from Ramat David to Nicosia in Cyprus with a 'rat trap' (a large wire metal container hanging out of the bomb bay) that contained the kit of a Spitfire Squadron. We were escorted by the 12 Spits formating on us and playfully making mock attacks. These squadrons were pulling out of Palestine prior to the ending of the mandate.

Although technically I was an air gunner I had never fired a gun in the air and and it seemed unlikely that I ever would. One day, on our way back to Ramat David from Egypt, I went into the rear turret to have a cigarette, it has air conditioning!

I pondered over this lack of experience, then an idea struck me. Taking out my .38 service revolver I double checked that I did have seven instead of six rounds, satisfied, I released the safety catch, pointed the revolver through the slot in the perspex and fired one bullet safely out to sea. Big Deal, I was now a qualified air gunner.

This tour of duty ended after just **13*** days on the 17th May 1948 and we departed Palestine on attachment to Shallufa.

26

OPERATION COOLER

On the 5th of July 1948 we took off from Shallufa on a 'secret' operation heading down the Red Sea en route to Khartoum where we stopped overnight, refuelled, and took off for Eastleigh in Kenya.

After a one night stop we took on board nine Jewish 'terrorists', who had been interned there, and five army armed guards. We flew them to El Adem in North Africa, stopping overnight again at Khartoum. On landing at El Adem we were surprised to see that the perimeter track contained a selection of armoured vehicles and a multitude of foot soldiers. It was obvious that the high security was protection against any possible terrorist activity. As well as the Lancasters there were a large number of Dakotas from Transport Command.

Unloading commenced and we found this extremely amusing. The Jewish terrorists were assisting some of the armed guards, who had been air sick, down the ladder whilst holding their rifles and kit for them.

On the 19th June we returned to Shallufa, and two days later to Luqa to resume A.S.R duties.

On 28th June we took part in FXM(48), a night exercise with the Royal Navy. Just 25 minutes after take off in TX263 we had to return to base when the T1154 transmitter caught fire. Transferring to PB305 we again took off and for almost seven hours searched for various ships of the RN, whilst flying fairly low over the sea. It was a very stormy night and extremely dark and we failed to find any of the 'enemy'.

The return to Luqa was at dawn and on calling Air Traffic Control we were advised which runway to use and were given visibility of one or two miles. Duke brought Q-Queenie down and made a very bumpy landing, so much so that we ground looped and came to a halt facing the wrong way up the runway. He was furious and berated ATC over the radio for the false visibility they had given. A cool and calm voice from the Controller came back and suggested he open his window. Our windscreen was opaque with dried sea salt from flying low during the storm and we were in bright morning sunshine. A red faced Duke made his apologies.

On August 9th we did an Assimilated Airborne Lifeboat Drop. These were aluminium boats equipped with sails and survival gear.

At this time my divorce was coming up and I used this as an excuse to get back home to see Betty. The Berlin Airlift had just started and I had to wait almost six weeks for an aircraft to get back home. This happened to be a Dakota with some thirty airmen on board. On landing at Lyneham we were told the aircraft was being scrapped as it had corrosion of the wing roots.

I was given 'compassionate leave' to enable me to attend court and my divorce went through quite smoothly.

Transport Command's Dakota discharging the 'terrorists' and guards.

27

SWINDERBY....again

Following my disembarkation / compassionate leave, at the beginning of October I was posted to No.2 A.N.S. at Middleton St. George where I did just two exercises in Wellingtons and then was posted again to Swinderby where I became a screen instructor. This was the third time that I had been stationed here.

All newly qualified aircrew had to be checked out in the air by an experienced operator in their particular skills. However, this was with brand new crews, real sprogs with very few flying hours. The rough part was that there were too few new trainee wireless operators so we screen instructors had to fly as one of the crew as an aircraft must not fly without a wireless operator on board.

On one occasion I did two cross country exercises of 2 hours 45 minutes and 2 hours 35 minutes, landing at 0525. Allowing for the time to park the aircraft, stow my gear in a locker, get back to the mess for a drink and meal, say an hour, it was 0630, I was airborne again at 0800 for another cross country of 3 hours 20 minutes duration. Pressure from the powers that be for the new crews to complete their training with the least possible delay completely disregarded the lack of trainee wireless operators and put lives at risk by overstretching the screen instructors who had to 'keep them flying'.

We registered a complaint and three of us acted as spokesmen, making our case to the Group Captain. He agreed and issued an immediate order for all screen Wop/Ag's to move into one wing of the Sergeants' Mess, and excused us from attending the C.O's parade on Wednesday mornings.

On Wednesdays we were allowed to sleep in as long as we liked up until 1200 hours and that area of the mess on that day was out of bounds to ALL personnel until after 1200 hours.

He also promised to persuade the Air Ministry to transfer more wireless operators in to relieve the pressure.

It was at this time that the Air Ministry took an unusual but in my opinion wise decision to recruit new pilots from existing air crew in the belief that, for example, a navigator who had flown 1000 or 1500 hours would be much easier to retrain to a pilot than a totally new recruit.

I submitted an application but having heard nothing after some eight weeks I called into A.M. in Kingsway whilst on a short leave and asked what the position was. They checked the records and stated that no application had been received and advised me to take this up with my flight commander who should have co-signed and forwarded it. On my return to the camp I raised the question with S/Ldr Smith who was overall in charge of the flying programme. He admitted that he had filed away the application owing to the pressure to pass the crews through. He asked me if I would sign on for 22 years on the condition that he would ensure I got on a pilot's course within a year. I refused, but offered that if he got me on a pilot's course within the next three months then I would sign on for 22 years and if I failed the course I would stay on as a Wop/Ag. He refused.

As my three year engagement was coming to an end I decided that enough was enough and at the end of October I changed my uniform for civilian clothes and left the RAF.

28

'CIVVIE' STREET

At the beginning of November 1949, with just eight years service, I once more returned to civilian life. My 'contract' with the RAF included four years on the Reserve List and this meant going back to various RAF camps for two weeks 'training' each year. This training required me to do 20 hours flying and keep up with my Morse and operating procedures. As I got paid by the RAF as well as my employer it was like an extra holiday. Because I was still young enough they asked me to extend my 'Reserve' by two years, but during that time I did not do any training.

After a short spell I joined Hoover Ltd. as a sales representative rising to area sales manager in three years. I think my early years as an errand boy helped me to be at ease when talking to strangers, a big plus in sales.

I married Betty in 1952 and we raised two children, four grandchildren and one great granddaughter. Set up my own domestic appliance company in Kent and after about seven years, sold out to a company in Bedford. I then accepted a post as manager of four departments in an independent department store in Cambridge. Seven years later I was 'head hunted' by an engineering company in Derby, appointed a director after ten years. I resigned later when they failed to keep promises of remuneration based on performance .

Then at the age of 53 I had a career change from selling to setting up and managing a training workshop under the YTS scheme on behalf of the Derbyshire County Council. This was for all the young school leavers who had failed to get onto employer's work experience schemes and was based in part of the Derby College of Further Education.

A college lecturer, having heard from someone that I was ex aircrew and had baled out, asked if he could see my Caterpillar badge. (If you saved your life with an Irvin parachute, you became a member of the Caterpillar Club and were given a solid gold engraved pin shaped as a caterpillar). I had to say no as I had never claimed mine. I followed it up the next day and found that it was still available and it was subsequently received. It is now attached, and sewn for safety, on a unique Lancaster tie which I wear on special occasions.

After the war, our crew made little contact and I finally lost touch completely. Like so many, getting a job, getting married, buying a house and raising a family was a full time task and there was a tendency to forget the war years.

I decided that I would like to make contact with my crew but the Secretary of the Caterpillar Club was unable to provide information about them and suggested that I contact the Bomber Command Association. This I did, joining the Association at the same time. In their October News Letter was an article on the unveiling of a memorial to 49 & 576 Squadrons at Fiskerton two months earlier in August 1987.

I wrote to the Vicar asking for any information. His reply put me in touch with Tom Gatfield the secretary of the 49 Squadron Association and I joined. Unfortunately none of my crew were members.

That November, on Remembrance Sunday, Betty and I attended the service at the Fiskerton Church to see the Squadron Memorial. There were a number of other veterans there from 49 and 576 Squadron (576 took over Fiskerton when 49 moved to Fulbeck in October 1944). After the service I walked out for a cigarette and was joined by another 4T9er and in chatting found that he had also been a PoW and had spent the whole time at Stalag 4B. (My first PoW camp.)

In response to my question, “I don’t suppose you knew my flight engineer, Alan Vidow”, to my surprise he did. Within a week I was in touch with Alan and with five other members of the crew a couple of weeks later. The missing man, Len Crossman, had been killed in a motoring accident in 1946.

Over the next few years Betty and I went to the Squadron Association reunions as well as the November Remembrance Services at Fiskerton, making many good friends at both. After retirement we planned an extended visit to Australia to see her cousin Margaret and husband Erle in Victoria, as well as a visit to Spud in Queensland. Unfortunately Betty became ill with cancer and after some extended treatment and set backs, Spud and his cousin Betty Kyle came to the UK for six weeks and spent over half that time with us. Betty’s health deteriorated and I lost her just six weeks short of a our 40th Anniversary on July 18th 1991. (She joked that it was my devious plan to avoid buying her a ruby !)

Betty had made me promise that I would go out to Australia and do what we had planned to do together. So in 1992 I made the arrangements, adding visits to cousins and other relatives in Australia, New Zealand and Canada. The trip lasted four months. I slept in 40 different beds, visited Singapore, Perth, (travelled on the Indian / Pacific Train to Adelaide), then by train, coach or air to; Melbourne, Lakes Entrance, Ballaratt, Canberra, Sidney, Brisbane, Cairns, Frazer Island, Auckland, Hawaii & Vancouver.

In 1996, I moved to a new small bungalow in Heage, Derbyshire and a combination of computing, amateur radio, DIY, renovating a motorhome and the 49 Squadron Association became my main interests which became a life line that saved me from ageing and vegetating.

29

CREW PHOTOGRAPH

Twenty years of searching had revealed no trace of the only known photograph ever taken of the whole crew of Nancy Pants. It was taken by the station photographer at RAF Fiskerton in November or early December 1943 during a stand down period. We had won the cleanest aircraft competition in 'B' Flight. Wing Commander Adams saluted us as the photograph was taken but we never saw it as we became PoWs shortly after.

Then one evening, (with a glass of malt in my hand) a miracle occurred. Don Henderson, a member of the 4T9ers rang me. During the conversation he raised the question of how often crews had their photographs taken officially. I explained that it only happened if there was some special reason, the crew had finished a tour of operations or had done something of special interest during an operation etc. I then told him about our photograph and explained the reason why we had never seen it. He responded with, "Well, I am sitting here looking at it."

It was a good job that I was sitting down... It was such a shock after all those years and I was extremely excited. I persuaded Don to post it to me the next day, then had a sleepless night when later the thought occurred that it might get lost in the post. I rang Don early the next morning but there was no reply. All day I sweated on the problem and eventually managed to contact Don when he got home from work. No, he had not posted it, "OK", I said, "Can I drive down and collect it?" He replied, "No I will drive up with it right now." My excited anticipation was unbearable.

Don duly arrived at 9.45 and handed me a 4" x 2" print. It was of the actual ceremony but was a snapshot obviously taken from the side, probably the adjoining dispersal, by someone with a personal camera. Don thought it was the official one as it was on Air Ministry photographic stock.

It was fairly common for the station photographic section to develop and print film from private cameras, especially for overseas members who had no access to this from home.

On the back of the snapshot are the names of the crew and in the case of four, including the Canadians, their home town. I guess that it was taken by another Canadian who knew them.

Don never told me where he got the photograph and I still do not know to this day. I had a negative professionally made from the print and the result is reproduced below, the only known photograph of Nancy Pants and crew.

L to R; Jack Scott (part hidden), John Young, Les Orchard, Alan Vidow, Ted Cachart, Spud Mahony and Len Crossman. There are also three of the ground crew just behind us but they, unfortunately, are unidentified.

F/O JOHNNY YOUNG (NELSON, B.C.)
F/O SCOTT (WINNIPEG, SASK.)
P/O ORCHARD (BRISTOL, ENG.)
SGT VIDON (LONDON ENG.)
" CACHART (BRITAIN)
" MAHONEY (AUSTRALIA)
" CROSSMAN (BRITAIN)

AND "NANCY-PANTS." (LOST 1943/44) 49 SQN

I believe the photograph may have been taken by a Canadian who knew the Skipper Johnny or navigator Scotty as, like others from countries abroad, they had access to film that was not available in the UK.

The night that I first saw the photograph, taken in 1943

30

RETURN TO BERLIN

This wonderful discovery led me into the minefield of research as I began to try and find out what actually happened when 'Nancy Pants' collided with the other Lancaster over Germany, and if possible, the identity of that aircraft.

At a Duxford Air Show in 2002 I met by chance a German Researcher and author, Michael Foedrowitz, who was there with his wife Marie. I was able to assist him with some information a few weeks later and emails were exchanged over the next few months. Michael, knowing my desire to return to Germany, invited me to stay with him and Marie. Further emails were exchanged and on January 1st 2004 I flew to Berlin where I was met by my hosts at the airport and driven to their flat.

For the next two days they took me round Berlin and we spent some time at the Commonwealth Berlin Cemetery... and

Marie, Ted and Michael in the Hotel Adlon, Berlin

it reminded me of the previous time I had set foot on German soil. It was so 'bloody' cold. There was almost an inch of frost on the grass and we soon discovered that our feet were ice cold and that it was creeping up our legs. On the night of January 3rd, the 60th anniversary of my previous visit, Michael said he had a surprise for me the next day. We set off in the morning in his car, which unfortunately had a faulty heater. We stopped for coffee and to get warm in the centre of Neubrandenburg. After another 1½ hours drive we pulled up at the gates of Trollenhagen, the Luftwaffe base to which I had been taken just 60 years previously on January 4th 1944.

Michael had told them of my 'previous visit' and I was duly invited as their Guest Of Honour on this anniversary.

We were met by Leutnant Ralf Hinkemeyer (who was my host and interpreter) and were ushered into the dining hall of the Officers' Mess and introduced to the Squadron Commander and the Base Commander. I presented Ralf with a hard back copy, inscribed and signed, of the 49 Squadron book 'Beware Of The Dog At War'.

In a minibus we toured the base but I saw nothing of the block of cells in which I had awaited the arrival of the rest of the crew. We visited the Flying Control which was built into the side of a hill and could not be seen from the air. It overlooked the single East - West runway.

The Meteorological Officer showed us the radar screen that covered most of Northern Germany and pointed out the huge cloud over Hamburg that was in fact a snowstorm that was heading our way. He then put on his hat, buttoned his coat and bid us farewell as he was going home! We also left, driving to the back of the administration block and Ralf opened one of a pair of doors. As I stepped through the threshold my skin tingled and hair stood on end as I recognised the staircase ...

"These are the stairs that I was taken up... the C.O.'s office... is at the top on the left," I said.

Ralph was surprised but pleased and we quickly climbed them and entered the office on the left. It was the outer office for his secretary but seemed smaller than I remembered. When I made this observation they confirmed that some years ago it had been partitioned off to create a new C.O.'s office and they used the original for an officers' meeting room. Photographs were duly taken... but I still didn't get my scout's knife back.

The drive home in falling snow and an unheated car needs

Sitting at what I believe was the same desk that I stood in front of when interrogated by the Station Commander on that cold morning, 4th January 1944. On the left is Ralf Hinkemeyer (now promoted to Hauptman) and alongside is the Squadron Commander, Oberstleutnant Reitz.

no description, your imagination will adequately cover that situation. Some amber malt was consumed on arrival at the flat which helped thaw us out.

The very next day, Michael and I returned to the cemetery where I made notes of the location of every 49 Squadron grave from the record book in the main entrance. We then walked along row after row, finding each grave, reading the inscription and ticking it off on the list. I forget exactly how many but I believe it was in excess of fifty. It was freezing, there was no wind and clear blues skies but oh so cold.

Ted at the Berlin Commonwealth War Cemetery

We returned to the flat and after an hour I was still shivering so Marie suggested that I had a bath.

Their bath was quite long, very deep and had no handles. The taps were on the wall above one side. I half filled the bath and climbed in, lay back and for the next half hour thawed out. Now came a problem... I could not get out. The long days of hectic activity had begun to take their toll, added to the excessive cold of that afternoon which had drained all my energy. I could hardly sit up and could not get a grip anywhere to be able to stand or even get into a kneeling position. Getting one leg over the edge, I tried to pull myself over the side but I kept slipping back. Eventually, after a more determined effort I managed to get up onto the side only to slip off onto the floor. It was a good ten minutes before I could pull myself to my feet using the radiator.

I went straight to bed and slept for well over nine hours. I was still feeling very weak and exhausted so settled for staying in pyjamas, wrapped in a blanket. I sat in an armchair in the lounge and had some coffee and toast. Just as I finished a young lady called at the flat, was invited in and lead into the lounge by Michael who introduced her as a reporter for a German National newspaper. She did not speak English so all her questions and my replies were interpreted by Michael. She described me as an elderly gentleman recovering from the effect of 'flu'.

The following day I bade farewell to Michael and Marie at Berlin Airport. On arrival at Heathrow, Colin Cripps (49 Squadron Association Researcher) was there to meet me and drive me to his home where I had left my car. A quick cuppa and I was on my way, despite being tired I was determined to sleep in my own bed that night... I left it thirty-six hours later!

The airbase at Trollenhagen, north of Neubrandenburg.
This aerial photograph was presented to me when I revisited the base as a Guest of Honour on the 60th anniversary in 2004.

31

RESEARCHING 'NANCY PANTS'

I now began in earnest to find the identity of the other Lancaster involved in the collision and where our own aircraft actually came to earth. The RAF Air Historical Branch provided me with the details of all 27 aircraft that were lost that fateful night. Of these 27, there were survivors from only 8 aircraft; their interrogation reports revealed that none of the 8 had been involved in a collision. Of the remaining 19:

DV401	QR-Z	Crashed at **0130** at Friesland
JB114	OL-Q	Crashed 6 Km east of Essen
JB355	OL-J	Crashed at **0315** 18 Km from the centre of Berlin
JB453	OL-F	Crashed at Blankenburg (no time recorded)
ND330	OL-O	Crashed at Wahrenholz (no time recorded)
JB459	NW-C	Lost without trace
W4780	AS-H2	Lost without trace
D5739	QO-Y	No info except 1 RCAF crew member buried in France
JB738	AR-T	Crashed **6 minutes** after take off
JA902	JO-D	Crashed in water that was later drained in Holland
JB123	PG-D	Crashed near Fallingbostel in Western Germany
JB747	PM-M	Crashed Zehrensdorf, 6 Km S.E. Zossen
JB310	GT-O	No known cause all crew buried in Berlin War Cemetery
JB553	GT-J	Presumed crashed over target
JB640	GT-V	Lost without trace. Wreckage found in East Berlin 1976
ND380	GT-T	Crashed at Reisdorf
JB681	DX-J	Crashed Luhme (Steinford (?) 20 Km east of Neustrelitz
JB727	EA-S	Crashed near Lessow 12 Km south of Neustrelitz at 0230
JB231	EA-N	Crashed 12.5 Km south east of Neustrelitz, approx 0230

Now, if as our mid upper gunner, Spud, reported, the cockpit of the other Lancaster struck our wing, it is extremely likely that the pilot and flight engineer would have been killed or seriously injured... with the probable result that out of control it would crash to the ground near to the collision. Two aircraft were identified, and could possibly be interpreted as aircraft breaking up in the air. This theory is reinforced by the German records that state 'some wreckage was found'.

The first real big break in my quest was the release of the British Interrogation Reports made and signed by all returning ex - prisoners of war from Germany in 1945... remember, we had to prove who we were.

Colin Cripps, (his uncle was killed on operations with 49 Squadron and is buried in Holland), spends countless hours at the Public Records Office at Kew, researching for both himself and for those who have a 49 Squadron connection. Colin managed to obtain copies of the actual interrogation reports for all seven of our crew. In answer to the tantalising question 'where were you captured?' - three had given Berlin (some 60 miles away from the collision.... but it was the target), three said Neubrandenburg (which was the large town that we passed through on our way to Trollenhagen) and Scotty, the navigator, said Neustrelitz.

Working on the assumption that, as a navigator, Scotty 'may' have actually known where he was! I contacted Hauptman Ralf Hinkemeyer at Trollenhagen. Armed with this fresh information, he visited Neustrelitz on my behalf. Here he was told of a retired forester who knew where in the forest a Lancaster had crashed. Frustratingly this trail went cold as Ralph was unable to make contact with him.

A few months later my spirits were lifted again when dramatic information was received from one of Colin's fellow researchers in Holland. Documents had been obtained from, of all places, the American National Archives. On 27 pages of 'liberated' German documents, 8 pages dealt exclusively with our Lancaster and crew.... I couldn't believe our luck!

Named were the different villages where five of the crew were individually captured. More importantly, it clearly stated that the Lancaster crashed between the villages of Godendorf and Wokuhl which are only a few kilometres apart.

Other pages gave details of various crashes and captives covering the same period. Most importantly amongst them were references to Lancaster EA-S (JB727) from 49 Squadron, stating that it crashed at 0230 hours and just some 12km from Nancy Pants' impact point.

After consultation with Colin Cripps and John Ward (49 Squadron Association President and Historian) we deduced from the relevant information that there were only two Lancasters that could possibly have been involved in the collision; EA-S (JB727) or DX-J (JB681) (57 Sqdn).

The RAF Air Historical Branch stated JB681 crashed at Luhme some 25km from Nancy Pants but does not give the actual time. On checking ORBs etc, we established that Nancy took off 33 minutes after JB681 and therefore should not have been in close proximity at any time.

I decided that a further visit to Germany was required. A few phone calls and Michael once again came to my aid by inviting me to spend a week with him. Ralf Hinkemeyer arranged for us to stay two nights at the Officers' Club (mess) at Trollenhagen. Apparently, when asking the Commanding Officer and Mess Manager he added "Ted was here before all of us !" - not only did the C.O. agree but I was invited to be their guest. (It pays to know the right people.)

I arrived in Berlin on Sunday night July 22nd 2007 and Michael and Marie met me at the airport. Unfortunately, due to a baggage problem, we lost most of Monday as far as research was concerned. On Tuesday morning we drove to Wokuhl hoping to find someone local who might remember where exactly Nancy came down. We met the local Vicar and family who were extremely friendly and invited us to join in their late al fresco breakfast. They tried to help by directing us to an elderly lady who had lost a son, two brothers, father and father in law in the war. Unfortunately, neither she, nor anyone else knew exactly where in the forest our Lancaster crashed.

Undaunted, we headed to a motor service station where we met up with Ralf and in convoy drove to Retzow in search of S-Sugar (JB727). Here I was introduced to Margarete and Heinrich Ross. Remarkably Margarete has tended the graves of the crew of JB727 and two graves of another Lancaster DV376 (50 Squadron), ever since she was a young girl.

Margarete led me into a very pretty cemetery.... there in a quiet corner stood five immaculately kept Commonwealth headstones. As I gazed upon the stones, the inscribed names of F/Lt Palmer and Sgt Camm suddenly hit me like a thunderbolt! For years, during many hours of research, these

Heinrich, Margarete, Hauptmann Ralf Hinkemeyer and me at Retzow

had been just names on paper.... but on this warm summer's day, a cold shiver ran down my back. After 64 years I was standing beside a fellow 49 Squadron crew.... who like us, on that cold night in January 1944 had departed Fiskerton bound for Berlin.... we may have even shared the same crew bus! Emotions began to well up inside me and my hosts, detecting my change in mood, left me to my quiet contemplation. Tears slowly began to fill my eyes as I became all too aware that 'but for the grace of God' these graves could well have been those of my own crew!

Ted at the graves of the crew of JB727 EA S-Sugar at Retzow

F/Lt Palmer and Sgt Camm each have gravestones both with the inscription "Believed to be buried here". On a third gravestones it states, "Four Airmen of the 1939-45 War, Royal Air Force, 3rd Jan 1944," and underneath are the words "Known by God". Here must lie the remaining members of the Palmer crew (note one member missing). The other two stones are for two crewmen from 50 Squadron who's Lancaster came down during a later attack on Berlin.

I came to Germany determined to find out if it was indeed Johnny Palmer's aircraft that collided with us that night.... as I stood by their gravesides, my heavy heart told me it was.

Pulling myself together, I braced up into the attention and with head lowered, I bade farewell to my fallen comrades and reluctantly departed this 'little corner of England'.

I presented Margarete with a bouquet of flowers with the deepest compliments of the 49 Squadron Association.

On the road again, this time to Luhme to see if we could determine the time that the 57 Sqdn Lancaster JB681 crashed. We met the Burgermeister, Wolfgang Duhm, who turned out to be an ex flight engineer on Heinkel 177 bombers. Michael had telephoned him in advance and he was able to give me a sketch (see photo) that he had made of the Lancaster (JB681) crash site. He was not there at the time of the crash but from witnesses he understood that the Lanc blew up when only 100 feet or so above the lake and crashed into the forest. The time of the crash remains unknown but he promised to check with other villagers and advise me if anyone knows.

It was very interesting (and ironic) to meet a member of an 'enemy' bomber crew. Heinrich related a very moving wartime incident to me which I found most poignant.

In February 1945 they were flying low over the Baltic sea when a B17, obviously in difficulties, ditched in the cold sea. The Heinkel circled over it and witnessed nine airmen scramble out and float away from the sinking plane supported by their 'Mae West' life jackets. A radio call was made to Heligoland for the Air Sea Rescue boat but because of the distance, one by one the airmen succumbed to the cold and drowned. When the ASR boat arrived they were all dead.

Two elderly flyers shooting lines! *Wolfgang, Ted and Marie*

It had been a very emotional day one way or another...memories of that day still touch me.

On Wednesday morning, Marie went to visit friends in Neubrandenburg whilst Michael and I drove to the village of Kittlitz to try and locate the farm where I was when the war

Christopher Becker and his father, farmers of 'The Farm' at Kittlitz

ended. After making numerous enquiries and being given various directions we arrived at a farm.... Some things looked familiar, was this where 500 PoWs had stayed?

It took a short time to get the orientation and to hear from the farmer that the tall barn had been altered and was now lower... but there was no doubt in my mind...I could even see in my mind's eye the Australian galloping around that field on 'my' captured horse! This 'find' was most exhilarating.

Ted in front of the farmhouse where he stood when finally released in May1945. The barn on right, although modified, is where we all slept.

(left) Ted pointing towards the barn, (right) Looking down the lane that I walked and met the German officer on horseback with his 30 troops.

Next morning we packed out bags, bade farewell to Ralf and drove to Godendorf once again in search of Nancy Pant's crash site. After a few enquiries we met Traute Lintov, a very pleasant elderly lady, whose property backed onto a lake. We sat lakeside in the sun as we discussed my search. She could not confirm the crash site but recalled that Mr Eckern, a local man, had been involved in the capture of a PoW in the village and had written a book which included the details.

Traute Lintov, Michaela and Marie lakeside at Godendorf

She telephoned a friend who had a copy of the book and arranged for us to call. We made our way to another small village and met the two ladies who invited us into their small 'castle' for coffee. Michael read the relevant chapter in the book and his (unedited) interpretation follows:-

Felix von Eckardt

„Ein unordentliches Leben
Lebenserinnerungen"

Düsseldorf, Wien 1976 Pages 106,107

"When we speak about the Volkssturm (Home Guard), I have to report that it had a forrunner in the country side, which was named, as I suppose, "Landwacht" (country guard). It was a sort of surveillance service during air raides, a protection against sabotage and similar things. Since that time I possessed a pistol. Once in World War II I became 'military active' with this pistol in my hand. One morning, when dawn started, my administrator woke me up, a real Berliner with the name Franz Gohlke, called the "old Johlke". He brought me toilsome out of my bed, because a day before one of our neighbors got a alcoholic sending, we exterminated...

Four men and our daghound „Mr. Knopp" were ready to go, because during the air raid in the past night on Berlin the flak had shot down a plane and the crew bailed out with parachuts. I thought the whole thing is a ferry tale and started to go ill humoured with other villagers. But it should be different. Suddenly we discovered a spot on a meadow, which appeared as an beautiful silk parachut when we came nearer. We gathered around astonishing and thinking all the same, as I suppose: how many beautiful and urgend needed shirts could be sewed out of this silk! But nobody relied on each other and so the chute was rolled up carefully and handed over a little bit later. In my daghound the hunting fever occurred. With the nose on the ground he was running here and there and finally he stood rooted on the spot and holded out barking in front of a large haystack. It didn't take long and a young man in a flyer uniform crawled out of the haystack. I asked him,with the mentioned pistol in my hand, to come down: "For you the war is over!" The laddie was not more then 20 years old and was freezing terribly. With some effort I succeeded, to bring my comrades calm, because of their bitterness they holded this young soldier responsible for the devastation of Berlin. Of course it was a ugly thought. But it was understandable because of the trouble and the awfull agitation, which Goebbels directed vers the enemy flyers. We villagers had countless opportunities to stand on a small hill watching the gleaming of the burning Berlin and listening to the roaring planes coming and flying off. Our village was situated some 90 km away from Berlin, but it was possible to find out the accurate quarter of Berlin attacked, illuminated by the "christmas trees". In those moments all the time I imagined the heart – rending pictures of the mothers running with their children to the air raid shelters, breathless pushing the perambulators, lugging a suitcase, trying to save the lives of their children and their owns. The threatening danger didn't impress me so deep but the humiliation to led the mothers run for saving the lives of their children.

Finally the young flyer, a canadien, sat in our living room. My wife gave the the wet and freezed through warrior a hot soup, which was forbidden by the way. I myself tried to start a conversation with him, but he remained quite taciturn. Only when I asked him, how often he already went with his bomber to Berlin, he answered laconically "One time to much". The military town major of Neustrelitz, who was informed by me, send a Wehrmacht vehicle to pick him up."

Was this Len Crossman ?

Some interesting information that came to light during this final search was the fact that all this part of North East Germany was a secret and secure zone. Captured allied planes were repaired here and made fit to fly again. It is believed that B17's were sent back with the bomber stream, carrying spies and saboteurs to be dropped by parachute into England.

Various secret war armaments were tested here and it was also the homes of Oswald Pohl and Heinrich Himmler plus many other Senior Nazis. Numerous SS troops were stationed and trained in the immediate locality. Parachuting into this region during the war was potentially an exceedingly dangerous occupation... I'm glad that I did not know this at the time!

JB231 Nancy Pants crashed between the villages of Godendorf and Wokuhl approximately 12.5 Km south east of Neustrekitz and 90 Km north west of Berlin *Photo Google Erath*

32

'Now this is not the end'...

Winston Churchill

To end this story here is difficult... so many questions remain unanswered and so many problems remain unsolved. Yet, to the vital question of which Lancaster actually collided with us that night... I am 99% convinced that it was EA-S (JB727). Based on the times of take-off and the times each crash took place, there can be little doubt.... but as yet it cannot be proven.

The one thing I do know for certain is that the German people that I met during my quest were absolutely delightful. Everyone was courteous and most obliging, giving freely of their time in an effort to help this curious English veteran.

One day, I'm certain that the place where N for Nan came to earth will be found. This noble Lancaster saved our lives... she suffered one hell of an impact, losing more than half her wing and one engine... yet still remained airworthy. She held together in a screaming dive long enough to allow the valiant efforts of our pilot and flight engineer to regain control. Then, whilst the skipper used all his skills, she remained stable whilst we all baled out safely.

Her final resting place will be in a woodland clearing which nature will have reclaimed after the ravages of the destruction suffered so long ago. The birds will be singing and shafts of sunlight will penetrate softly through strong branches.... and there, hanging high up in one of the tall trees will be a small tattered rag doll called 'Nancy Pants'. She will be swinging gently... just like she always did above Johnny's head in N-Nan's cockpit!